THE MAKING OF URBAN AMERICA

Tracing the rise of the American city from colonial times to the present day, this book explodes the myth of America as a land of small towns and farms. A vivid picture of the mistakes of the past, the problems of the present and the challenges that must be met in the race against time to save America's cities.

BOOKS BY BARBARA HABENSTREIT

CHANGING AMERICA AND THE SUPREME
COURT

THE MAKING OF URBAN AMERICA

ETERNAL VIGILANCE
The American Civil Liberties Union in Action

The Making of Urban America

by

BARBARA HABENSTREIT

**JULIAN
MESSNER** New York

Published simultaneously in the United States and Canada by
Julian Messner, a division of Simon & Schuster, Inc., 1 West
39 Street, New York, N.Y. 10018. All rights reserved.

Second printing, 1971

Printed in the United States of America

ISBN 0 671-32321-0 Cloth Trade
     671-32322-9 MCE

Library of Congress Catalog Card No. 73-123182

CREDITS

The Autobiography of Malcolm X. Copyright © 1964 by Alex Haley
    and Malcolm X; Copyright © 1965 by Alex Haley and Betty
    Shabazz. Published by Grove Press, Inc.
East Hampton History. Copyright 1953 by Jeanette Edwards Rattray.
    Privately published in East Hampton, Long Island.
Manchild in the Promised Land, by Claude Brown. Copyright 1965,
    The Macmillan Company.
Negro Migration During the War, by Emmett J. Scott. Arno Press
    Edition 1969.
The Story of Sag Harbor, by Nancy Boyd Willey. Long Island Herald
    House, 1939.
Them Was the Days, by Martha Ferguson McKeown. University of
    Nebraska Press, 1961.
Twenty Years at Hull House, by Jane Addams, originally published in
    1910, by The Macmillan Company.
The Welsh in America, edited by Alan Conway. University of Minne-
    sota Press, 1961.

CONTENTS

INTRODUCTION

In 1800, America was a small agricultural country. Its people lived mainly on farms or in the rural towns and villages that dotted the eastern coastal region.

A little more than a century later, the country had expanded across an entire continent and turned into an industrial giant. Its people lived mainly in large cities, and the small farmer was well on his way to becoming a vanishing breed.

America made the change from a rural country to an urban-industrial one faster than any other nation in the world. Changes came so rapidly that Americans still tended to think of themselves as basically "small-town people" long after the majority of them were already living in the large cities.

The image Americans had of themselves and their country was very much like the quiet, pastoral scenes on Currier and Ives Christmas cards, or in the cheery Norman Rockwell illustrations that graced the covers of the *Saturday Evening Post* for so many years.

Americans didn't want to think of themselves as city people because, in a philosophical sense, they didn't really like cities very much. Many American leaders, from Thomas Jefferson on down, praised the virtues of rural life while warning against urban evils. The antiurban bias was probably a relic of America's Puritan heritage, which tended to equate sinfulness with big-city life.

But ironically, and almost against its will, America became the largest urban nation in the world. Today, about 70 percent of the American people live in urban areas. Of the 30 percent left in rural regions, only about 5 percent actually live and work on farms. The rest live in small towns and villages.

The process of urbanization and industrialization began along the eastern coast, where the first large seaport cities sprang up. They became the lively social and cultural centers of the young nation.

As people migrated west, they built new towns and villages farther into the heart of the country. Some of these towns became large trading centers, where the settlers could get the finished products of the East in exchange for the raw materials from their new farms. Other towns served as supply stations for those who were pushing still further westward. It wasn't long before these busy little towns became cities, far removed from their old frontier ways.

As the people spread throughout the land, new methods of transportation were needed to link the growing country together. Out of this need came the steamboat and the railroad, which in turn spurred the growth of heavy industry.

Americans were quick to adopt new and better ways of doing things. Faced with a need to produce more manufactured goods for the growing western markets, and handicapped by a shortage of skilled labor, they turned to new machinery and mass production techniques.

They were equally inventive on the farms. On the great plains of the Midwest, where pioneers found a strange new soil that didn't respond well to the old farming tools, they came up with new machines that were far more efficient. In this way, the mechanization of American farms began.

All the while, immigrants kept coming. The earlier ones tended to spread out on farms and in rural areas, buying up acres of cheap fertile land. This was what they had come to America for. Here they could own their own land, while in Europe they toiled for others.

But during the second half of the 19th century, large masses of immigrants started pouring into the cities. This was partly because the land was filling up. By 1890, America had no huge unsettled tracts of land left. The frontier was gone, and the best lands had already been taken.

By the early 1900s, the cities were swollen with immigrants. In addition, the farm population was declining as people left the land and headed for the greater opportunities of the city. The growing use of agricultural machinery was reducing the number of people needed on the farms.

Between 1910 and 1920, America became an urban country. It was also a highly industrialized world power with a complex economy. But politically and socially, people were not yet ready for such changes. National problems were still being treated with small-town remedies, stressing action (or inaction) by local governments rather than the federal government.

When the Depression struck in 1929, people first realized how interdependent the economy had become. Under President Franklin Roosevelt, the national government started tackling the problems of a full-grown urban-industrial nation.

Today, the aging cities are in the midst of a different kind of crisis. The post–World War II migration of poverty-stricken Negroes from the rural South to the cities has created large, festering slum ghettoes in almost every urban center. At the same time, the white middle class has been leaving the inner cities and heading for the surrounding all-white suburbs. The society is polarizing into two separate camps—the poor and the black of the inner cities, and the white and well-off of the suburbs. We are approaching apartheid.

In the long run—or perhaps even in the short run—the survival of the cities as we have known them may depend on the ability of the American people to solve the monumental problems created by discrimination and poverty.

Faced with a crisis affecting the basic structure of our society, it is no wonder that people often look back nostalgically to the "small-town America" of the 19th century, and wonder how and why we ever got to where we are today.

part one ▰▰▰▰

The Vanishing Farmer

1

A SMALL-TOWN NATION

The crowd began forming early in the morning around the little railroad station, even though the train wasn't expected for several hours yet. It was a very small station, only six by eight feet, and could easily have been mistaken for a cast-off outhouse. But newcomers to the scene seemed fascinated by it. Almost all of them looked it over and walked back and forth inside as if to try it out. The uneven, rough pine floorboards creaked loudly under their heavy footsteps.

By noon, just about everyone in town was lined up around the station and along the newly laid railroad tracks, waiting for the big event. For this was 1895, and the railroad company had just completed its tracks through the easternmost tip of New York State. Three small, rather isolated farming and fishing towns—East Hampton, Amagansett and Montauk —would now be linked directly with that giant metropolis 120 miles to the west, New York City.

On this particular day, May 10, the first passenger train was due to come through. But the crowd in East Hampton had a long wait, for the train was late. Most of them had stretched out on the grass or on blankets when the sound of a far-off whistle brought them to their feet. Though they could hear the train, they couldn't see it until finally it chugged around the rear of Henry Filer's house and crossed Newtown Lane.

For nine-year-old Hugh Filer this was a very strange sight, because the train went right over the spot where his house had stood just a few months before. His whole house had been picked up and moved out of the way, closer to the street, so that the tracks could be laid properly. Now the train practically ran through Hugh's back yard.

Jeremiah Baker also watched the train with mixed feelings. Every day for almost 50 years he had driven a mail and passenger stagecoach from Amagansett to the bustling port town of Sag Harbor ten miles away, passing through East Hampton as he went. As he entered Main Street he would always blow a bugle to announce his arrival. But now his bugle would give way to the train whistle, for the railroad was taking over his job of delivering the mail. By 1900, Jerry Baker's stagecoach would be out of business.

That first train into East Hampton was greeted with wild cheers and shouts from the waiting throng. Many of them climbed onto the train and bought tickets to the last stop at Montauk. Others, especially the children, ran alongside the train as far as they could before it outdistanced them.

The scene was much the same in Amagansett, although the people there had not been as eager to have a railroad as their neighbors in the larger town of East Hampton. They kept a lot of cattle in Amagansett, and the people were afraid the noisy, smoky trains would disturb their cows. But East Hampton had raised more than $8,000 to buy rights of way and to send delegates to New York to persuade the railroad to extend its line. Once the railroad agreed, Amagansett reluctantly went along with the plans.

The people of Amagansett had good reason to be apprehensive, for the coming of the railroad was to bring about more changes than these little rural towns had experienced during the whole 250 years of their existence. For one thing, the railroad would bring many "city folk" into the towns, strange people with odd-sounding names and accents, shocking clothes, "loose manners" and "looser morals." There would be the Irish, the Poles, the Italians and the Jews—all having customs and ideas far different from those of the local people, who came from Puritan stock and had remained isolated from other ethnic groups.

The area still had much of the flavor of early New England, despite the fact that it was part of New York State. Located just across Long Island Sound from Connecticut, the villages were Puritan in spirit, and their backgrounds were similar to those of many New England towns.

East Hampton had been founded by a small band of Englishmen who were religious Non-Conformists. They had lived peaceably in England until 1634, when the government began to make life difficult for them because of their religious beliefs. They were persecuted for the next 14 years until finally, in 1648, they set out to build a new settlement for themselves in America.

With the help of other Englishmen who had already settled in Connecticut, they bought about 30,000 acres of land on the eastern end of Long Island from the Montauk Indians. The price they paid, according to the deed of purchase, was "20 coats, 24 hatchets, 24 hoes, 24 knives, 24 looking glasses and 100 muxes." (Muxes were tools that could be used in making wampum, the Indian money.) The total value of these goods was a little more than 30 pounds sterling, making East Hampton more costly than Manhattan Island. The agreement was dated April 29, 1648.

The little settlement grew over the years, with houses

springing up along a wide street about one mile long. This was Main Street, the heart of the town. In summer it was shaded by large elms and sycamores that grew on either side and formed a thick leafy arch overhead. On the southern end of the street was the Presbyterian Church and the village burying grounds, where old eroded stones marked the graves of the first settlers. There were names such as Mulford, Hand, Barnes, Osborn, Hedges and Dayton—names that gave the town its identity through streets like Dayton Lane, Hedges Lane, Barnes Hole Road and Stephen Hand's Path.

Descendants of these settlers had branched out to farm the surrounding countryside. They cleared more land, built new homes, went into business, married their neighbors and raised children—all within a short radius of the original town and the little villages that had sprung up nearby.

The families became intertwined with each other, and there was a saying that you had better not insult anyone from the town because if the person wasn't related to you he was sure to be a relative of a friend or neighbor.

This sort of inbreeding meant that East Hampton, like many other rural towns and villages in America, was a very homogenous community. The people all stemmed from the same kind of background, they practiced the same religion and on the whole they shared the same values and beliefs as their neighbors. Their thinking had been shaped by the townspeople who came before them, and they passed on the same attitudes to those who came after.

Theirs was the so-called Puritan ethic of white Anglo-Saxon America—an amalgam of beliefs that placed a high moral value on such things as hard work, thrift, independence, chastity and self-denial, an unquestioning belief in God and going to Church on Sundays. These were the values that dominated American thinking throughout most of the country's history, and they remained strongest in the small towns and rural areas, where they were not diluted by close contact with other ethnic and racial groups.

Since most Americans lived in such rural areas until the first quarter of the 20th century, this Puritan ethic formed what came to be known as "the American way of life"—although in fact it never was the "way of life" in the large cities, with their mixtures of religious, racial and ethnic minorities and their potpourri of ideologies.

In this respect, East Hampton was far more representative of America during the 18th, 19th and early 20th centuries than a city like New York, for its history embodied the mainstream of American thinking. How East Hamptonites felt about religion, government, politics, foreigners and such was the way the majority of Americans felt at that time. What was important to them was important to most people who lived on the farms or in the small towns and villages across the country.

One of the most important things to the people of East Hampton and places like it was religion. The earliest settlers had left their homeland and traveled across an ocean for the sake of religious freedom, for their whole lives centered around the worship of God. Although they paid lip service to the idea of separation of Church and State, in reality there was no separation, at least not within the town of East Hampton.

For 200 years East Hampton had only one church—the Presbyterian—which was supported by everyone. The Town Trustees governed the church as well as the town. They hired the ministers, paid their salaries and managed church property. They even took care of such things as having the church floor swept, ringing the bell and paying someone to make sure the children behaved while their parents were attending the long services.

Church and State were finally separated in East Hampton in 1848, when the board of trustees of the First Presbyterian Church was set up to manage church affairs. The transition was accomplished despite a good deal of opposition from people who preferred the old way.

Seven years later, a church of another denomination—St. Luke's Episcopal Church—held its first services in the town. This church was founded by an "outsider" who had first come to East Hampton in 1846. He was somewhat of a mystery to the townspeople for he never told anyone where he had come from or why. He used the name "John Wallace" (later discovered to be an alias), and he was apparently wealthy for he donated large amounts of money to charity and was served by a valet. He was a favorite topic of gossip, especially after a mystery novel, *The Shadow of John Wallace*, was written about him. After his death in 1870, St. Luke's Chapel was open only in the summertime for the next 30 years.

There were a considerable number of Methodists in East Hampton by the middle of the 19th century, but they had to attend services in Amagansett's Methodist Church because East Hampton did not have one of its own.

Episcopalians and Methodists were readily accepted by the Presbyterian majority in East Hampton. But the story was quite different with regard to Catholics.

The first family of Catholics—Francis Martin, his wife and five children—found their way into East Hampton in the 1760s, but they didn't stay long. They were Acadians who had been exiled from Nova Scotia and left penniless. Martin did whatever work he could find, and the townspeople helped the family somewhat. But records show that in 1764 the town trustees paid David Fithian seven shillings for "carting Francis Martin to Sag Harbor." There were no more Catholics in East Hampton for some time after that.

By mid-19th century, however, Catholics began to trickle into East Hampton, even though they were treated with cool disdain by the Protestant townspeople. The nearest Catholic church was in Sag Harbor, seven miles away. Early Sunday mornings, the East Hampton Catholics could be seen trudging down the dusty Sag Harbor road on their way to mass. They would also hold masses in people's homes and, as their numbers grew, the congregation sometimes spilled over onto the lawn where onlookers could see them kneeling and praying.

The most eminent member of this group was Julia Gardiner Tyler, widow of the former President and a member of the Gardiner family, one of the founding families of East Hampton. Mrs. Tyler had converted to Catholicism late in life, and she gave the Catholics a certain amount of respectability in the eyes of the Protestant townspeople.

A notation in the diaries kept by Miss Fanny Huntting of East Hampton summed up the town's attitude pretty well: "July 24—Sunday [1881]. This morning I counted sixty persons coming from Mass which is held every other Sunday in the house of Patrick Lynch. I think the Catholics feel pretty well set up, as Mrs. ex-President Tyler is of that denomination and is a regular attendant at Mass."

St. Philomena's Roman Catholic Church was built in 1894 to serve the 60 Catholic families living in East Hampton. The Catholics were there to stay, and the Protestants didn't really mind so much by then (although their Puritan ancestors would probably have been horrified).

Although the people's attitude towards religion had broadened considerably over the years, their feelings about government did not change so very much. The first settlers in East

Hampton brought with them the English system of law and the tradition of representative government, which had its basis in the Magna Carta. But at the same time, the Puritan settlers had been treated so badly by the English government that they were mistrustful of men in authority. In setting up their own government, they chose three men to serve as judges on a court that would handle all legal matters. But in order to prevent the judges from becoming too powerful, their decisions were not necessarily final; they could be appealed before a meeting of the whole town. In this way, the people kept ultimate power in their own hands, and everyone had a direct voice in the government.

Open ballots were the rule at these town meetings (also called General Court). Everyone had to attend and vote one way or another or else they would be fined. Voting was considered a duty more than a right.

Although they still considered themselves Englishmen and acknowledged England's authority over them, they resented interference from a far-off government in which they were not even represented.

East Hampton had its own particular complaints against England. By the early 1700s, whaling had become the most important industry on the eastern end of Long Island, with whale oil the major product. The Governor of New York colony slapped a large tax on whale oil and required all whalers to be licensed. This enraged the people of East Hampton, but the Royal Governor just ignored their protests. Finally, they decided to take their complaints directly to London. Their emissary on this mission was Samuel Mulford, a prosperous East Hampton whaler who was also a member of the New York General Assembly.

In 1716, at the age of 71, he sailed off to England on behalf of his fellow townsmen. Having heard many stories about the notorious London thieves, he sewed fishhooks into his pockets. He actually did snag a would-be pickpocket this way, and the resulting publicity brought him to the attention of the King, who granted him a direct audience. The whale oil tax was repealed by royal decree, and Mulford returned home triumphantly. From then on, he was known as "Fish Hook" Mulford. However, the Governor of New York was furious that Mulford had gone over his head, and saw to it that he was expelled from the General Assembly.

This type of warfare with the royal governors continued for decades, with the grievances mounting and becoming increasingly difficult to bear. England did not remain sympathetic, so that by 1776, East Hampton was wholly committed to the revolutionary cause. Although the British won the battle of Long Island and occupied the area for the duration of the war, many of the men in town escaped to Connecticut, where they could continue fighting.

When the war ended, the American colonies were on their own at last. Misrule by England and its royal governors had hardened the people's distaste for strong governments. Those in East Hampton were left with a suspicion of governments that were not subject to their close control. They felt that the more removed a government was from the people, the less power it should have over them. This led them to favor a weak central government and stronger state governments. But most of the power, they felt, should remain on the local level so that the various towns and villages could govern themselves according to their own particular needs.

This attitude persisted through the years, and was eventually translated into the philosophy: "That government is best which governs least." This was essentially the philosophy of the Republican Party until well into the 20th century, and East Hampton has remained strongly Republican to this day.

Political habits vary widely from region to region and even from village to village, but on the whole, most rural people throughout the nation have tended to be more conservative politically than their city counterparts. They are particularly wary of strong, active governments that attempt to experiment with economic or social reforms. In part, this is because rural people in the past had less need of government protection than city people, whose livelihoods depended so much on economic and social conditions.

Most people in East Hampton, for example, worked for themselves and owned some property. Although few were actually wealthy, almost all families at least owned their own homes, with enough land to raise some vegetables for home use and to keep some cows and chickens. For many, farming was also their business, since the land was particularly well suited to such crops as potatoes and corn.

As one old farmer of the last century reported: "My farm gave me and my whole family a good living on the produce of it, and left me one year with another $150, for I never spent more than $10 a year which was for salt, nails and the like. Nothing to eat, drink or wear was bought, as my farm provided all."

Fishing was also a popular occupation, since the town was bordered by a bay on one side and the ocean on the other. Many of the local fishermen would set off in their own small boats early in the morning, returning later in the day to sell their catch of striped bass, flounder or red snappers right from their boats, while the sea gulls hovered above waiting for leftovers.

There were shop keepers and craftsmen, as well as professional men who had received their education elsewhere and then returned to their home town to open up a practice.

Many people did a combination of things—a little farming,

a little fishing and perhaps some carpentry on the side. They lived close to the land and the sea, and though life wasn't easy, there wasn't much real poverty either. By and large, if a person worked hard and developed a few skills, he could make out all right. Most of the people never experienced the long, grinding hours of factory work or understood the need of workers to band together into unions. Theirs was a non-industrial world in which men did not have to rely much on their society to get ahead.

Self-reliance, ambition and a little Yankee common sense were thought to be all that was really needed. Laziness was not tolerated. In fact, it was looked upon as a sin. In colonial times, the shiftless were actually expelled from the town. The first such expulsion took place on October 7, 1651, when the town fathers issued the following decree: "It is ordered that Daniel Turner shall within the space of ffortnite eythe sojurne in some ffamily or bee a servant to some man or else Depart the Towne." Turner apparently left, for his name did not come up again.

Other expulsions followed in the years to come, for the unemployed or shiftless were despised by the hard-working Puritans. This attitude lingered through the centuries, although the penalties against those who didn't do their share were softened from expulsion to ostracism.

But the attitude towards those who were incapable of working was quite different. Widows, especially those with young children, were looked after by the townspeople in a variety of informal ways. In early days, the town officials saw to it that a widow had a cow, some pasture land and wood for her fire. In addition, her house was kept in good repair.

When serious illness or some other disaster struck a family, the townspeople almost always took up a collection to help tide the victims over their difficulty.

The feebleminded were also looked after informally. Families usually took care of their own less fortunate relatives. They had large houses and ample land, so that several generations of assorted relatives might all live together under one roof. In his memoirs, *Life in East Hampton*, Hugh Filer talked about his childhood home, recalling: "The two bedrooms upstairs were occupied by my two uncles, George and Thomas, both bachelors. My uncle George was always my favorite, but I was rather fearful of uncle Tom, whose worst besetting sin was rum. He lived with us until I was 4 years old, when he became too unmanageable and my father built a small house for him beyond our barn and put him in it. He lived there for a few violent years (two to be exact) when demon rum made short work of him. He was always a kindly man except when in his cups when he became insane and finally died in August, 1892."

On the whole, East Hampton was a close-knit community, and the people could be quite cold to outsiders. There was a saying that it was easier for a foreigner to become a naturalized citizen of the United States than for an outsider to become "naturalized" in East Hampton.

This was particularly true regarding people of other ethnic groups, such as the Irish, Italians and Poles. Some Irish had begun drifting into East Hampton in the 1870s. There were no Italians in the area until around 1895, when the railway laborers came in to lay the tracks. Young Hugh Filer's reaction to these Italians was probably typical. He said, "During the course of construction, the laborers, 'Ginnies' we called them, would stop at noon and eat their dinner by our property. Some would even come and buy milk from us. Their meals usually consisted of a hunk of baloney and half a loaf of bread which they unwrapped and just knawed on like a dog. They were quite a peaceable gang and no very serious fights

occurred, though they would continually jabber among themselves, and, all in all, we got along very well."

Some of the Italians stayed behind and settled in the area,
and gradually they came to be accepted.

But for the people in East Hampton, as in most other rural
areas of America, accepting new people, new ideas and different ways of life did not come easily. The isolation of rural
living fostered a sense of clannishness, because the people of
one area did not usually have too much contact with people
in other areas. Although New York City was only 120 miles
away—barely a three-hour trip today—East Hampton was
hardly influenced by it at all. Many of the modern conven-
iences that were commonly used in the city had scarcely been
heard of in East Hampton. One old-timer recalled a trip to
Brooklyn in 1894 to visit an aunt. He said, "It was that trip to
her house that I saw, and used, my first real bath tub. She
also had gas lights which I had never seen, which seemed so
wonderful."

Before the railroad came through, a trip to the city involved long, exhausting hours of travel, usually overnight.
Roads were bad, especially country roads—muddy when it
rained, impassable when it snowed and always rough and
bumpy. There were no movies, radio or television to help
spread ideas from one region to another. Out-of-town news
in the local papers was often weeks old, sometimes even
months old.

The most cosmopolitan influence on East Hampton up to
the beginning of the 20th century was the port of Sag Harbor,
seven miles away. This was a big whaling town and the commercial hub of eastern Long Island. Its streets were crowded
with sailors of all nationalities and colors who unloaded their
money in the bars and night spots that lined the narrow
streets. When men from East Hampton wanted a night out,

they would go to Sag Harbor for the kind of entertainment that was not available in East Hampton. For one thing, there was no liquor in East Hampton because every April at the town meeting the people voted to keep the town "dry." Sag Harbor much preferred to be "wet."

The port was like a small city in atmosphere and in its variety of inhabitants. It was never as puritanical as East Hampton, for many different types of people made it their home. Its industries attracted foreign-born workers of varying religions, so that Irish Catholics, Baptists, Methodists and Jews lived there side by side while East Hampton was still almost entirely Presbyterian.

In *The Story of Sag Harbor*, Nancy Boyd Willey gave a good description of the port town in mid-19th century, when its population was about 4,000. "In lower Main Street, lined to the dock with stores, taverns and warehouses, there was the irresponsible life of a seaport town. While on upper Main Street, in fashionable homes, there was a brilliant society, and arrogant youth skimmed through the streets with a horse and cutter. The silk hat, the Fiji Islander, the tankard of rum and . . . the church bell."

It was a place quite different from sedate East Hampton, just a few miles away, and even more different from Amagansett, a little further east. Amagansett was probably among the most clannish and conservative towns anywhere. A New York newspaper described it as it was in 1894, when the residents were still very much like their Puritan ancestors in "stern morality and strict integrity" of character:

"The main street in Amagansett is 150 feet broad, lined with magnificent elms, each house surrounded by extensive ground; no house pretentious but all of them comfortable. None is rich here; none is poor.

During the past 40 years it is said that but two families have moved into the village. Immigrants are not sought for; emigration is unknown. The population is fixed and reliable except as varied by birth and death. Gravestones in the 200-year-old cemetery register the same names as the living bear.

In those days, each of the three towns had its own distinct personality and style, even though they were just a few miles apart. Bad roads and slow forms of transportation kept the towns separate, so that they were closed-in and self-contained. The people turned mainly to their immediate neighbors for their day-to-day needs, entertainment, gossip and exchange of ideas.

In East Hampton, the most common type of entertainment was a community get-together. This included such things as strawberry festivals, clambakes, barbecues, church suppers and sleigh rides. An especially festive event was a house raising. This took place when the roof of a new house was finished and ready to be set on the building. Although a man could build a house by himself or with the help of a few workers, many hands were needed to hoist the roof into place. Most of the men in town would pitch in to help, and after the work was done there would be food and drink for all. This is probably how the expression "raising the roof" came to mean having a wild or boisterous celebration.

Dancing was not really accepted as proper in East Hampton until about the 1870s. Even then, some of the old-line Presbyterians continued to object. Card playing was not permitted among the young people at all until late in the 19th century. Courting took place under the most protected conditions, and even then it was not necessarily based on romance. Many young men in town simply "jumped the fence" for their brides—that is, they married the girl next door in order to keep the properties together. Divorce was practically unheard of. Until the beginning of the 20th century, there was only one known divorce in the history of East Hampton. It occurred in 1648, the year the town was founded.

Wives were expected to be hard-working and thrifty, and to make many of the goods needed by the family. They knitted and sewed, churned butter and made such things as soap and candles. These items were used sparingly. In the evenings, only one candle was used for the house. If there were guests who stayed late, a second candle might be lit. But after that one burned out, everyone sat in the dark. If a woman was known to burn more than one candle at a time, she was considered wasteful and extravagant.

Such habits limited the ways in which people could spend their leisure time at night. They couldn't do much reading by the light of one candle, but then they were not particularly bookish people. In many homes, the only book was the Bible (and perhaps a mail-order catalogue). People wanted their children to learn the three R's, but beyond that there wasn't too much stress on formal education. For one thing, the children were needed to help on the farms, with the fishing or with the household chores. In early times, boys attended school only in the beginning of winter, which was the slack season. The schools then were run privately, and the teachers charged a small fee.

As the town prospered, the wealthier residents hired help to work the land and sent their children off to the private schools. The children of the poor had almost no schooling at all until 1812, when New York State passed a law for the support of public schools. Even so, it was very rare for a poor child to get more than the basics until much later in the century.

This, then, was the way many rural people lived prior to the 20th century. Thomas Jefferson strongly believed that this was the best type of life—the best setting to ensure the survival of liberty and self-government. He felt that if the country grew too big and too industrial, with power centralized in a federal government, the people would lose control over their own affairs and might fall victim to tyranny.

Jefferson hoped that America would remain an agrarian country, with the majority of people living in small towns and villages. But even in his lifetime, industrialization and urbanization were beginning. By 1800, large cities had sprung up along the eastern seaboard, and life in these places was taking on a far different shape and color from that in rural America.

2

BIRTH OF THE CITIES

It was a glorious afternoon in New York City. The air was clear and crisp after the heavy rains of the day before. But there were still some enormous puddles in the streets, so that every time a horse and cart clattered by, the people had to scramble out of the way to avoid being splashed. One big rainfall could make a mess of New York's streets for days. The Common Council kept talking about the drainage problem, but as usual they weren't doing anything about it.

Three fashionably dressed young ladies, with their skirts held safely above the messy cobblestone streets, walked along briskly until they came to Longworth's Shakespeare Gallery. After paying the one-shilling admission price, they went inside.

The ladies weren't particularly fond of art, but they were interested in fashion and had come to see the newest styles from London. Each month, Longworth's received from abroad the "London Gallery of Fashion," which featured two elegant colored prints of what the best-dressed Englishwomen were wearing that month. Longworth's framed these prints and hung them up. They always attracted large numbers of female patrons.

Even though America had just fought one war with England and would soon fight another, New York society still imitated London in matters of culture and refinement. The American elite may not have wanted to be English, but they did want to live in the English style.

Fashions were not the only attraction at the gallery. Longworth's was known for its collection of beautifully illustrated prints of Shakespeare's works. There was also Gilbert Stuart's famous portrait of George Washington, as well as five other portraits of the first president; two portraits of John Jay, Governor of New York; and one portrait of Thomas Jefferson. Political figures seemed to be very popular subjects for artists at the beginning of the 19th century.

The three young ladies lingered at the gallery for a while and then left. As they walked down the street chatting to each other, they hardly glanced at the various stray animals that were roaming about. Animals were a common sight on the streets of New York at that time. Dogs, cows, goats, chickens and especially pigs wandered about freely. But as the city grew and traffic increased, the animals became more of a nuisance. Sometimes they were even a menace to public safety. In 1802, the *Weekly Post Boy* reported the following bizarre incident:

"Yesterday afternoon as a genteel person was walking along Beekman Street, he was suddenly attacked by a cow. . . ." The man died, and the episode aroused new demands to get the animals off the streets.

The Common Council had already passed several laws prior to 1800 permitting people to keep any pigs or goats they found on the streets, but still the stray animals continued to multiply.

For one thing, most people believed that the pigs performed a useful function by eating the garbage that was regularly swept into piles in the streets. Actually, they scattered more than they ate, making garbage collection more difficult.

Such were some of the problems of a growing city at the start of the 19th century. New York, with its veneer of sophistication and elegance, was still in many ways a primitive, crude place to live. It was the largest and gayest of the American cities, but English officials who were assigned to it before the Revolution looked down on it as a provincial backwater. It couldn't even compare with such cultural centers as London, Paris or Vienna.

They felt the same about the other large urban centers in America—Philadelphia, Boston, Baltimore and Charleston. In 1800, these were the only cities in America that had more than 10,000 inhabitants; 97 percent of the American people still lived on farms or in small towns and villages.

The five largest cities had many things in common. Most important, they were all seaports with harbors deep enough and safe enough for oceangoing vessels. It was through these five ports that the young American republic exported its own raw materials to foreign markets, and imported whatever the country couldn't produce itself. Trade was the big occupation then, for industry was still in the infant stage.

The ships that sailed into these ports brought far more than just material things. They brought news of what was happening in Europe and elsewhere. They brought word of the latest in politics, business, art, music and the theater; they brought new, sometimes revolutionary ideas about government and religion; they brought the most advanced theories in medicine and science. In short, they brought civilization to a country that was just emerging from the wilderness and was separated from the rest of the world by vast oceans.

These ports were America's only link to the Old World. The news and gossip that buzzed through the port cities eventually spread to the rural areas. Traveling salesmen and traders would load up their wagons in the cities and then head for the countryside to sell their wares—and to pass on all the gossip as well. They provided a valuable service, for newspapers of the day were very slow to report out-of-town events.

Although the five major seaports were all cultural centers as well as commercial centers, there were many differences among them. For one thing, they had each been settled by different types of people, and their diverse origins were still very apparent.

New York was the only city that was not originally settled by the English. The Dutch founded it in 1609, calling it New Amsterdam. Since it had a fine natural harbor at the mouth of the Hudson River, the Dutch thought it would be an ideal trading center. Traders could sail up the Hudson in their small boats to barter with the Indians for furs. Then they could return to New Amsterdam, where their goods would be loaded onto larger ships bound for Europe.

Furs were avidly desired by the well-to-do of Europe, and merchants could never get enough to keep up with the demand. Many fur-trading posts sprang up along the Hudson River, and soon New Amsterdam was doing a bustling business.

As the town grew larger, it began to resemble the city of Amsterdam in Holland. The Dutch built sturdy brick houses with roofs of colorful tile that they brought from Europe. Small gardens and orchards surrounded most dwellings, and the town contained several windmills and a canal.

In atmosphere, too, the city resembled its namesake. The Dutch were a jovial people who enjoyed holidays, and they kept up their Old World customs of giving gifts on Saint Nicholas Day, and of dressing up in their finery to call on all of their friends and neighbors.

When trouble developed with the Indians, the Dutch built

a wall of sharpened logs across the width of Manhattan Island to protect the northern border of their settlement. The road running along that wall was named Wall Street. Today, that same street is the financial hub of the entire country.

From the first, New Amsterdam was a very cosmopolitan settlement. Sailors from all over the world came and went, and as many as 18 different languages could be heard, in addition to Dutch.

After the English defeated the Dutch in 1664 and turned New Amsterdam into New York, the city became bilingual. English and Dutch were spoken about equally, with a variety of other languages in lesser use. In later years, the existence of two main languages created grave problems in the development of the city's public school system.

There were also two main religions in the city—Anglican and Dutch Reform.

This meant that, from very early times, New York was a blend of two cultures, Dutch and English. This alone made it more cosmopolitan and urbane than the other large cities along the Atlantic seaboard. The upper classes indulged in many elaborate social affairs, including formal balls and dinners and amusements such as cockfighting, hunting, coaching and skating. Poorer people could find their pleasures in the city's many taverns, which served as meeting places and social centers.

Philadelphia, on the other hand, was far more sedate and straight-laced than New York. One Pennsylvania Senator confessed, "To tell the truth, I know no such unsocial city as Philadelphia. The gloomy severity of the Quakers has proscribed all fashionable dress and amusements."

However, during the decade of the 1790s, when Philadelphia was the official capital of the United States, the city glittered with social activity. The presence of so many silk-

stockinged government officials, foreign diplomats and aristo-
crats with powdered wigs overshadowed the Quaker simplic-
ity and made Philadelphia a social rival of New York.
But after the seat of government was moved to Washington, Quaker influence dominated once again. Music, dancing
and the theater, which had flourished during the 1790s,
declined as the city returned to its more intellectual pursuits.
The Quakers were a serious, sober people who had come to
America from England to escape religious intolerance. Under
the leadership of William Penn, they founded the "City of
Brotherly Love" 100 miles up the Delaware River. Their little
settlement was open to all peaceable men, regardless of
religion.

The promise of tolerance attracted many different groups
—Irish Quakers, Anglicans, Presbyterians, Baptists and Catholics. Trade and commerce thrived, so that by the time of
the Revolution, Philadelphia was the second largest city in
America.

Its growth rested largely on its exports of food grown on
Pennsylvania's rich farming lands. Banking and finance also
got an early start in Philadelphia as the Quakers became more
absorbed in business than in religion. However, their material
drive was tempered by a concern for scholarly and humani-
tarian pursuits. Scientists, doctors, philosophers, astronomers,
writers and artists were warmly received and assisted by
Philadelphians.

When the town was just 10 years old, the Quakers established a school in which poor children could receive a free
education. The William Penn Charter School was opened in
1701 to "all children and servants, male and female, whose
parents, guardians and masters be willing to subject them to
the rules and orders . . . the rich at reasonable rates and the
poor to be maintained and schooled for nothing."

The school accepted Negro children as well as white, and taught more than just the three R's, including literature, languages, arts and sciences. Many other schools sprang up after that, all supported by private donations.

In contrast to the openhearted tolerance of the Philadelphia Quakers, Boston's early Puritans were a fanatical, autocratic group. Anyone who dissented from their views was expelled from the colony. The burning of "witches" flourished in this stern New England town where the Puritan clergy ruled.

The colony was founded in 1630 by the Puritans of the Massachusetts Bay Company. Faced with a barren, rocky soil, the settlers quickly turned to the sea for their survival. They became excellent shipbuilders and fishermen. Their catches of cod, mackerel and haddock were salted down and shipped to Europe. Fish of a poorer quality were sent to the West Indies, where wealthy planters bought them as food for their slaves.

Boston rapidly became the commercial hub of the New World, and held her lead until the middle of the 18th century, when she was outstripped by New York and Philadelphia.

As a major seaport, Boston couldn't remain closed to other religious groups for very long. Little by little, other sects settled in the growing city, so that its Puritan spirit gradually mellowed.

Nevertheless, the Puritan desire for orderliness lingered on. Lawbreakers were quickly punished by a public whipping or a day in the stocks. Town officials were vigilant in their suppression of thievery, violence and prostitution, so that Boston had far less crime than the other large seaports.

The Puritans also had a strong sense of public responsibility and were the first group to provide for the needy at public expense. In other cities, the poor were aided by private charities.

Schools were also set up with public funds, for the Puritan faith required worshipers to read the Scriptures. A well-educated clergy was particularly essential, so the Puritans founded Harvard College in 1636 to train men for the ministry. Every settlement in Massachusetts colony was taxed for the support of the college. Public secondary schools were also begun, and later on elementary schools as well.

By 1690, Boston was spending half of its tax revenues on public education. The city had a higher literacy rate in the 17th and 18th centuries than any other place in the Western world.

Girls, however, were left out. They got only the three R's in "dame school"—a place where a woman would teach other children along with her own.

One English visitor to Boston wrote in 1719, "Humanity and knowledge of letters flourish more here than in all other English plantations put together."

Despite their Puritan heritage, Boston's wealthy classes developed a taste for luxurious clothes and exquisite household furnishings. They liked to have their portraits painted, and they bought clavichords and fiddles so they could play music in their own homes. There was a great deal of wealth in the city, and the Boston rich became noted for their elegant stone and brick mansions.

Several hundred miles south of Boston an entirely different urban culture was developing—an aristocracy based on slave labor—in Charleston, South Carolina.

Built in 1683 by a small band of English settlers, the town developed very slowly. Twenty years after its founding it still had only 1,100 inhabitants and hardly anything of value to export.

Then, in the early 1700s, a number of English planters from the West Indies began migrating to the port town. They brought their slaves with them, and established a West Indian-style plantation system in the surrounding area. The swampy soil and subtropical climate was perfect for growing rice, which became the main crop for export.

But in the summertime, the swamps and marshes of the rice lands also bred malaria, so the planters moved their families into town, where the disease seldom struck. They built fine town houses with sheltered balconies, or "galleries," where they could enjoy the sea breezes. When the weather grew cooler, they would return to their plantations.

In time, it became a social custom for South Carolina planters to maintain sumptuous town houses in Charleston, where they spent most of their time. Overseers managed the plantations and slaves did all the labor, so the planters were free to enjoy their leisure. Unlike the Puritans and the Quakers, the Southern planters were not troubled by the fear that idleness was sinful; they enjoyed it thoroughly and were very good at it. In devoting themselves to gracious living, they went to concerts, balls and the theater. The racecourse was especially popular, and in 1800 the first golf course in America was built in Charleston.

Religion was taken lightly in this sophisticated city, where the inhabitants were of varying backgrounds. In addition to the English planters from the West Indies, there were also French Huguenots, French Acadians, Scotch-Irish and South Germans. More than half of the population were Negro slaves. In 1800, Charleston had just 8,820 whites out of a total population of 18,924.

There was little opportunity for the rise of a stable middle class. Slaves were trained for many crafts, so it was very difficult for the competing white artisans and craftsmen to earn a comfortable living. Only planters and merchants prospered. For the most part, the poor remained poor.

It was also almost impossible for the poor to receive an education in Charleston. All public services were neglected in the city, since the rich were expected to provide everything for their own families and be responsible for their slaves and workers. Children of the wealthy were educated in private schools, and needy relatives were supported by others in the family. There was no public sewerage system or municipal water supply. Streets were not paved, and there was no public street lighting. In matters of public responsibility, Charleston lagged far behind the northern cities until late in the 19th century.

Standing in between Charleston and the cities to the north was Baltimore—a blend of Yankee energy and Southern geniality. In business matters, Baltimore men were as ambitious, enterprising and aggressive as any of their Northern rivals; but after working hours, their style was strictly Southern.

During the 18th century, the slave-owning, tobacco-growing Maryland planters had looked down on the Baltimore merchants, no matter how prosperous they had become. But by the early 1800s, money finally overshadowed these early distinctions. Planters and merchants together formed a genial, fun-loving upper-class society that was particularly fond of horse racing and cockfighting.

Baltimore grew spectacularly during the last decade of the 18th century. In 1790, she was not yet a major city, but by 1800 her population had doubled to 26,000 and she was larger than the older cities of Boston and Charleston. By 1830, she overtook Philadelphia to become the second largest city in the United States.

Her rapid growth was due largely to the shrewdness and

foresight of her merchants; her exports of wheat and tobacco and the skill of her shipbuilders. Baltimore clippers became famous all over the world because they were built to hold large cargoes but were very speedy despite their weight.

In most matters of public responsibility, Baltimore was fairly progressive. However, the city was very slow to set up a good educational system. Even though tuition was low in the private and parochial schools, many Baltimore children remained illiterate.

By 1800, each of the five major cities in the United States had developed its own distinctive style and culture. Yet the similarities of urban living—whether in rocky, harsh New England or the warm, languid South—far outweighed the differences. A wealthy Bostonian could feel right at home in the high-ceilinged drawing room of a Charlestonian merchant. They might talk about fine wines, English politics or the newest scientific discovery. Worldly events were part of their lives, no matter which city they lived in.

Discomforts and problems of city living were also part of their lives. All the large cities were plagued with the troubles that arise when large numbers of people are crowded together —crime, poverty, poor housing and sanitation, etc.

New York's problems were fairly typical of any large American city at the start of the 19th century. Just as in all the other ports, immigrants were constantly streaming into the city. Many of them were poor; they were unfamiliar with city ways; often they didn't know the language; they needed a place to live; they had to find jobs.

The city could be quite cruel to its newcomers. Many charlatans and swindlers frequented the docks waiting for the boats to arrive so they could cheat the immigrants out of whatever valuables they had.

Most had very few. City commissioners in the early 1800s

reported that the rising costs of keeping the poor stemmed
from the fact that "many of them, having paid their last
shilling to the captain, are landed destitute and emaciated."
This was particularly true of the Irish, who were the poorest of
the immigrants at that time.

By 1802, the cost of caring for the needy had risen to
$34,989. It was the single highest item in New York City's
budget. Many of the poor were housed in the public almshouse, although some lived outside it and received direct aid.
All the large cities maintained an almshouse for the poor, but
some were supported by private donations rather than public
money.

Politicians, too, took advantage of the immigrants. On the
eve of a local election in 1802, one high-ranking political
figure had a group of 200 immigrants naturalized all at once
—just in time for them to vote for him for re-election.

Housing was another problem. Although many buildings
were put up quickly in the years following the Revolution,
they could not keep pace with the demand. Older houses,
built to serve one family, were subdivided into rooming
houses and packed with poor tenants. People squeezed into
run-down wooden shacks and shanties that created alarming
fire hazards. New York had several bad fires during this period, although they were not as bad as the huge blaze which
nearly gutted Boston.

Mainly to protect the city from fire, New York passed its
first slum clearance law on April 4, 1800. This gave the city
the right to buy and tear down houses that endangered the
health or safety of the city.

Like the other large cities, New York was a place of great
contrasts. Extreme wealth existed side by side with extreme
poverty; magnificent stone mansions were only blocks away
from dirty, foul-smelling slums. Such extremes were far less

visible in rural areas, where the people were neither so wealthy nor so poor.

In New York, the rich lived very well and made no effort to mask their sumptuous, extravagant way of life. Wealthy merchants and landowners were at the top of the social ladder. They threw lavish balls and banquets, and drove through the streets in ornately decorated English coaches drawn by four or even six horses. The ladies wore fancy hairdos, costly silk gowns and huge hats, while the men dressed in velvet or satin suits with ruffled shirts, knee breeches and shoes with elaborate buckles.

Their houses were magnificent, some of them actually resembling palaces. One such mansion, built a little later in the century by Dr. S. P. Townsend, cost about $200,000. It contained tiers of galleries and 60 Corinthian columns going up four floors to an exquisite domed roof.

A softly lit chapel occupied the third and fourth floors. It was lined with stained-glass windows and contained an elaborate altarpiece showing the baptism of Christ.

For lighter moments, the house also came equipped with a gymnasium and a "bowling saloon." The bathrooms, too, were not neglected. They were furnished with gilded nymphs and juvenile angels. For the art gallery, Dr. Townsend commissioned some of the leading artists in Italy to paint 20 pictures at a cost of $1,000 each. The marble fireplaces were also imported from Italy, at a cost of about $400 each.

This was a time when great fortunes were being made in the city. A young immigrant named John Jacob Astor was learning the fur business from the Quaker Robert Browne and from the Jewish merchant Hyman Levy. During the next half-century, Astor became the wealthiest man in America.

In 1810, another ambitious New Yorker borrowed $100

from his mother, who kept a small nest egg in the family
clock. He bought a sailboat and began ferrying people and
goods from Manhattan to Staten Island and back again. By
the end of his first year in business, he was able to return the
loan to the family clock, and had earned an additional $1,000.
Cornelius Vanderbilt had made his start.

Only the wealthy had enough leisure time to do much
traveling in those days. A round trip to Europe took three
months. A journey from New York to Boston by stage could
take anywhere from four to ten days at a cost of about $10.
Even a trip to Philadelphia involved an overnight stopover
in Newark, while a journey to Albany took two days. Stage-
coaches made regular runs to these cities from New York
several times a week, so that anyone who had the time and
the endurance could travel from city to city. The upper classes
did travel a lot, so that the elite of each city usually got to
know each other.

Despite so much wealth, New York was not a clean or
healthy place to live. Water from the public wells on each
corner was so vile that anyone with a little money purchased
drinking water from the private Tea Water Pump.

On August 24, 1798, the *New York Gazette* complained:
"Water drawn from any well within the city is generally too
full of filth and poison to be drunk by any person who regards
either delicacy or health."

Eventually, an aqueduct was built to bring water into the
city from the Croton River. However, the new system wasn't
completed until 1842, so the people of New York had to live
with their polluted water for a long time.

The condition of the water was at least partly responsible
for the epidemics of yellow fever that broke out regularly.
There were terrible epidemics every year between 1819 and
1822. Many people fled the city during these sieges, for there

was no protection from the disease. But the poor usually had no choice; they had no place else to go, so they stayed. Many of them died. All the port cities were afflicted with these recurring plagues of yellow fever.

The filthy condition of the streets also aided the spread of disease. There was no department of sanitation. People put their garbage out on the streets for the pigs to eat. Twice each week, householders were required to sweep the rubbish from the front of their houses into big piles in the streets. Then, once a fortnight, the city sent around oxcarts to tote the garbage away. The wealthy paid to have their garbage removed regularly by private collectors, but the poor had to wait for the oxcarts. In the summertime, the odor from the slum areas was particularly bad.

Even in these early times, the cities had traffic problems. More than 2,000 horse-drawn carts, coaches and private carriages rattled along the cobbled streets each day, making a continual racket.

In this bustling, crowded city, crime was always a problem. Many rough, unsavory characters came and went on the ships that docked at the harbor. Thieves, adventurers and prostitutes lurked around the waterfront area, and people frequently complained that the streets were not safe after dark.

In the years following the Revolution, New York was particularly prone to riots. In 1788, the state militia had to quell rioters who were protesting the medical practice of using dead bodies for experiments. This became known as the Doctors' Riot. In 1793 an outraged mob destroyed two houses of prostitution, and the same thing happened again in 1799. In the latter riot, the state militia was needed again.

In ordinary times, city constables patrolled the streets during the day, and at night the "city watch" (patrol) took over. These nightwatchmen were often recruited from the unemployed, and many were criminals themselves.

In very early times, they walked the streets holding a lantern on the end of a long pole. Each hour they called out the time. Later on, when public street lamps were set up on every block, the watchmen no longer needed their lanterns. As darkness descended, the lamplighters would make their rounds lighting up the city. However, in order for the city to save money, the lamps were not lit on nights when the moon was expected to be out.

Punishment of criminals was very severe in early years. For crimes such as robbery, forgery, housebreaking or arson, even a first offender would be hanged. For lesser crimes, a man might receive 39 lashes on his bare back, or he might be locked up in the stocks or branded. Imprisonment was rarely used except as a punishment for debtors.

On March 26, 1796, New York City adopted a new penal code in which it abandoned corporal punishment. It was the first municipality in the nation to make such a reform. Criminals were no longer whipped or branded; instead they were sentenced to hard labor in the state penitentiary. The death sentence was given out only for such grave offenses as murder, treason or stealing from a church.

The new penal code was hailed as a major step forward by humanitarians. However, the state prison filled up very quickly this way; by 1802, three-quarters of all convicts in the state penitentiary were from the city of New York. This only added to the city's reputation among out-of-towners as a "wicked, godless den of thieves."

It was true that the city had become much more "godless" since the Revolution. Growing numbers of people were casting aside the traditional religions and turning to such new beliefs as Deism, Unitarianism and Universalism. They started to rely more on reason and less on faith. Sabbath laws were openly disobeyed, and the pious were shocked to see children playing and skating on Sundays.

So many inhibitions were abandoned that by 1803 the Common Council found it necessary to ban nude swimming off lower Manhattan between 6 A.M. and 8 P.M. Council members said they were shocked by the "vast numbers of the youth and many of those of more advanced age who indulged in the indecent practice of swimming or playing and sporting in the buff on Sundays."

The growth of secularism also resulted in greater tolerance for people of all faiths. Before the Revolution, Catholics were banned from New York City. Under a law passed in 1700, any Catholic priest found in the city would be jailed for life.

The law was finally repealed in 1784, but even then Catholics could not hold public office in New York. Under city law, public officials had to renounce their allegiance to all foreign kings, potentates and states—ecclesiastical as well as civil. This meant that Catholics could not take office unless they renounced their allegiance to the Pope. However, they could worship freely, and by 1794 New York had its first Catholic Church. By 1806, there were 10,000 Catholics in the city.

Jews fared much better under colonial rule. They had their own synagogue by 1728, although they were denied political rights until after the Revolution. However, by 1812, there were still only about 500 Jews in all of New York.

The main religions were Dutch Reform and Episcopalian and, to a lesser extent, Presbyterian, Methodist, Baptist and Lutheran.

By 1800, New York City's population had reached 60,489, making it the largest city in America. Of the inhabitants, 54,122 were whites, 3,499 were free nonwhites and 2,868 were slaves.

But slavery was on the way out in New York. The 5,000

or 6,000 immigrants who poured into the city each year were forming a large laboring class that worked very cheaply. It became more economical to hire them than to use slaves, who had to be housed, fed and clothed. Furthermore, even though the immigrants were poor, many of them were skilled craftsmen and artisans who had learned their trades as apprentices in Europe.

At times there was even an oversupply of labor, resulting in periods of unemployment. In January, 1797, 600 idle journeymen, mechanics and tradesmen appealed to the city for help because they were going hungry. They asked to be given city jobs temporarily, until times got better.

A few labor unions got started around this period, and a particularly strong one was the printers' union. In 1805, the cordwainers' union started to build up a fund that could be used to help its members in case of a strike.

Much the same was happening in the other cities. A propertyless working class was getting larger and becoming more dependent on society. If business in the city was bad, jobs became scarce and people went hungry. City laborers had no land on which to grow their own food; they had to buy it. They didn't own their own houses; they had to pay rent. Unlike farmers, they couldn't get by without money to purchase the necessities of life.

However, this was still preindustrial America. Although urban life and rural life were already very different, the rift was to grow much wider once the Industrial Revolution took hold.

3

AMERICA BECOMES INDUSTRIALIZED

In England, the Industrial Revolution was already in full swing by the 1780s, especially in the textile industry. English men, women and children were laboring long hours in dreary factories to turn out more cottons, woolens and linens than any other country in the world. No one could compete with England because no one had the new textile-making machinery that was being used there. These machines could spin thread and weave cloth, and were run by waterpower.

Knowledge of how to make this machinery was practically a state secret in England. Parliament passed laws forbidding anyone to take any plans or models of machines out of the country. The export of machine parts was not allowed. People who had been trained in textile production were not even allowed to travel out of England.

Enforcement of these measures was very strict. All ships and passengers leaving England were thoroughly searched to make sure that no industrial secrets were being smuggled out of the country.

What's more, England kept flooding the United States with very low-priced manufactured goods, so that American industries couldn't really get started. This kept the new republic in a state of economic dependence on England, even after the Revolution. America still supplied England with raw materials in exchange for manufactured goods, just as in colonial times. Even such basic items as cloth, buttons, shovels, paper, rope and plows had to be imported. America seemed destined to remain an agrarian country that would have to rely on other nations for most of its manufactured needs.

But one day in 1789, a ship from England sailed into New York harbor carrying a number of immigrants. Among them was a penniless 21-year-old who was dressed in shabby clothes and carried only a small, tattered suitcase. His name was Samuel Slater.

Poor as he was, Samuel Slater had one asset that was worth millions—he knew how to put together all the machinery that was needed for running a textile mill.

At the age of 15, Slater had become apprenticed for a six-year period to the owner of one of the first English textile mills that was using modern machinery. The boy was an excellent worker and had a photographic memory. By the time he was 21, he knew the exact shape and size of every part of every machine in the mill.

But opportunities for a poor boy in England were limited, and it was unlikely that he would be able to start his own business there. He felt that if he could only get to America, he could earn a fortune.

But Slater was among those who were forbidden to leave England because of their technical knowledge. If he wanted to get out, he would have to sneak out.

He decided to disguise himself as a farmer, dressing in country clothes and affecting the speech of a rustic. All his knowledge was in his head, so he didn't have to smuggle any plans or blueprints out of the country. He only had to smuggle himself out.

His disguise worked, and he left England safely. But when

he reached America, he found it wasn't so easy to get started there either. He took a low-paying job in a small shop in New York while looking for someone to back his ambitious dreams.

Quite by chance, he heard of a factory owner in Pawtucket, Rhode Island, who was trying to build a cotton-spinning machine propelled by waterpower. Slater wrote to the owner, saying, "I can give the greatest satisfaction in making machinery."

The owner, a Quaker named Moses Brown, sent the following reply: "We hardly know what to say to thee. But if thou wilt come and do it, thou shall have all the profits over and above the interest of the money they cost and the wear and tear of them."

Slater went to Rhode Island, and by 1791 he had set up a complete replica of the English textile mill in which he had worked. His machines spun great quantities of yarn very quickly, and the mill was a tremendous success. Soon, other New England mill owners were copying the machines that Slater had built. A modern textile industry was taking shape in New England.

However, these mills used so much raw cotton that in just three years the supply ran out. Moses Brown and Samuel Slater had to shut their mill because they couldn't get any more cotton to feed into their machines.

Not much cotton was being cultivated in the South then because it was so uneconomical. Before cotton could be sold for spinning, it first had to be cleaned. Raw cotton was speckled with green seeds that clung tenaciously to the cotton fibers. If a slave worked all day removing the seeds by hand, he could still only clean about a pound of cotton. The supply simply couldn't keep up with the new, heavy demand.

At this point, a man named Eli Whitney happened to be

visiting friends on a Georgia plantation. He had just graduated from Yale, and was on his way to a tutoring job in the
South.

During his stop-off, he became aware of the problems
Southern planters were having in trying to increase cotton
production. Cotton grew wild over most of Georgia, so if a
fast way of cleaning it could be found, planters could make
enormous profits.

Whitney loved to tinker with machines, and during his
visit he came up with a simple little device that changed the
history of the South. He called it a cotton "gin" (short for
engine).

It took him just ten days to make the machine. The device
consisted of a wheel with teeth that drew the raw cotton
through narrow slits. The seeds couldn't fit through the slits,
so they fell out on one side and the clean cotton came out
on the other.

By using the gin, one person was able to clean as much as
50 pounds of cotton a day. Within a few years, almost every
Southern planter was growing cotton. It became the main
cash crop of the South. In 1794—just one year after Whitney
invented the gin—the cotton crop was up from five million
pounds to eight million. By 1800, production had reached 35
million pounds. By 1805 it was 70 million, and by 1825 it had
soared to 225 million pounds!

Now the Northern textile mills could get plenty of cotton.
Moses Brown and Samuel Slater reopened their mill. Other
textile factories sprang up all over New England, because the
area had plenty of waterpower for turning mill wheels and
was densely settled, providing a ready market for the manufactured cloth. This set the pattern for the growth of industry
in the North and the spread of huge cotton plantations in the
South.

Cotton required a long, warm growing season. It couldn't be grown up North. Furthermore, a great many field hands were needed to plant, pick and clean such huge amounts of cotton, so that slavery became far more necessary in the South just when it was dying out in the North. Many historians believe that slavery would have died out in the South, too, if not for the invention of the cotton gin.

Everyone was making money from cotton. Everyone, that is, except Eli Whitney.

Whitney had got a United States patent on his invention, and he opened a workshop in New Haven, Connecticut, to turn out cotton gins. He picked New Haven because he thought there were many skilled craftsmen there who could help him produce his machines. By himself, he couldn't possibly make enough cotton gins to supply all the Southern planters.

However, he was wrong. Skilled labor was very scarce in New Haven at that time because so many workers were heading west for the frontier. Their skills were needed to help build new settlements, and they could get their own land for almost no money.

Whitney found that the only workers left were the unskilled or poorly trained. They had so much difficulty learning how to make the cotton gins that Whitney produced very few.

The Southern planters couldn't wait. They started making their own cotton gins, which they copied from Whitney's original. Even though Whitney held the patent on the device, the patent laws were only a few years old and it was very hard to enforce them. Whitney would have had to spend all his time in court to protect his rights.

One of Whitney's problems was that his workers couldn't master all the skills that were needed to produce a complete cotton gin. Each worker had to first saw the wood to make a

box; then he had to make a wheel and cut teeth into it; then
he had to make the crank to turn the wheel, and so on. Each
worker made an entire gin by himself; that was how the
handicraft system worked, whether the product was cotton
gins or shoes or chairs.

In desperation, Whitney tried something else. He divided
the labor, so that each worker had to master only one skill.
One man sawed all the wood; another nailed it together into
boxes; another made the wheels; another notched them.

This system worked better. Each laborer worked much
faster than before. But there was still a problem. The different parts of the cotton gin didn't always fit together right
when they were made this way. Then time was wasted while
pieces were redone.

Finally, in 1798, Whitney closed his workshop. He was unable to make any profits from his invention. However, he had
learned some invaluable lessons. He knew that the division of
labor could work very well if only there was some method of
getting all the parts to fit together smoothly. He tackled this
problem and soon solved it by inventing different kinds of
"jigs."

A jig is a mechanical guide for a tool. The simplest kind of
jig is a ruler. Anyone can draw a straight line with a ruler.

Whitney invented far more complex jigs that could be used
as guides in operating machinery. He made jigs that stopped
a tool automatically when it had made exactly the right size
cut. He made clamps to hold things in exactly the right position, and tools to make exactly the right size hole. In short,
he found he could make machines with jigs for every proce-
dure, so that workers did not have to rely on the "rule of
thumb."

Items that were produced this way came out exactly the
same size and shape each time, and their parts were inter-

changeable. If three guns were made from the same machines, the barrel of one gun would fit either of the other two. This was something entirely new, and people could not believe it at first.

By using his new machines and dividing the labor, Whitney was able to produce thousands of muskets for the United States Army. These muskets were a vast improvement over previous guns. Since the parts were interchangeable, soldiers could carry spare parts with them and repair a broken musket right on the battlefield.

Whitney's method had other advantages, too. He didn't need highly skilled workers to do the job, nor did he have to employ great numbers of men. The machines made it possible for fewer men to produce more goods more quickly than ever before.

Whitney made a fortune producing muskets, not cotton gins. Other factory owners were quick to adapt his techniques for their own products. This became known as "the American system."

It was particularly well suited to this country at that time because labor was in short supply. Workers were heading west, so the Eastern factory owners replaced them with machines.

Furthermore, all sorts of manufactured goods were desperately needed. The Napoleonic Wars and the War of 1812 had totally disrupted trade. America couldn't get any more imports from England or France, and was forced to produce goods for herself.

New types of towns—industrial towns—grew up around the new factories. They flourished mainly in New England. Although a variety of goods was produced, textile manufacturing dominated most of the towns.

Life in these places was very different from life in the

average rural community or in the cities. People crowded together within a short radius of the mill in which they worked. They had to, because the only way they could get to work was on foot. The mill whistle sounded at six in the morning and at six at night. With a 12-hour working day, there wasn't much time left for traveling back and forth from work. Tenements surrounded the factories. Sometimes 10 or 12 families squeezed into houses built for two or three.

Although these towns were small, they had many of the problems of large cities without the opportunities and variety of real urban living. They had problems with crime, sanitation and housing. There was a great deal of disease, and the death rate was very high compared with that in other towns or cities.

The streets were filthy, and sanitary conditions kept getting worse. By 1875, the Massachusetts Bureau of Labor Statistics revealed: "Holyoke has more and worse tenement houses than any manufacturing town of textile fabrics in the state. . . . The sanitary arrangements are very imperfect, and in many cases there is no provision for carrying the slops from the sinks, but they are allowed to run wherever they can make their way. Portions of yards are covered with filth and green slime, and within 20 feet, people are living in basements three feet below the level of the yard."

Under such conditions, disease flourished. In Holyoke, infant mortality soared to 312 deaths for every thousand babies under one year old—a rate of about 31 percent.

The workers were poor. Most of them were immigrants who had recently arrived in the country, without money or skills. In Massachusetts, most of the immigrant workers were Irish. They were largely illiterate and knew nothing of American ways.

People in these towns were directly affected by economic

cycles. When there was a depression in the cotton industry, mill workers were laid off. The Panic of 1857 hit these towns very hard. Hunger was widespread. Those with a little money left the area, usually heading west. The poorest stayed behind.

Among the towns that developed this way were Bridgeport, New Bedford and Naugatuck, Connecticut; Manchester, New Hampshire; and Holyoke and Fall River, Massachusetts.

While the industrial towns were developing in the East, other towns were springing up further inland, beyond the Appalachian mountains. These were the river towns, Cincinnati, St. Louis and New Orleans.

The area west of the mountains had not been safe for settlement until after the defeat of the Indians of the Ohio country in 1795. Then the settlers started coming in larger numbers, although the trip was very difficult. They had to cross the Appalachians by wagon, and then switch to rafts or riverboats when they reached Pittsburgh, Pennsylvania, located at the headwaters of the Ohio River. From there they floated down the Ohio in search of good places to settle.

Many of them stopped at a small outpost high on the banks of the Ohio called Cincinnati. This was about 450 miles downstream from Pittsburgh, and had first been settled in 1788. By 1803, the town had about 800 inhabitants.

The land surrounding the town was very rich and fertile. Settlers who farmed the land grew large surpluses, which they brought into Cincinnati to be loaded onto riverboats. The cargoes were then sent downstream to New Orleans, 1,500 miles to the south.

The journey was treacherous, and many merchants lost their entire loads of cargo when the riverboats hit a sandbar or got torn apart by submerged logs. Sometimes the river froze, and produce piled up and rotted in Cincinnati warehouses. Other times, heavy rains and thick mud made it impossible for farmers to bring their produce into town. Then the merchants had no goods to export. Nor could they sell their supplies of household items to the farmers.

St. Louis, located on the west bank of the Mississippi River, faced the same difficulties as Cincinnati, for both towns lived by river trade.

But there was one overriding problem that plagued both towns and slowed their growth. This was the difficulty of importing goods.

Although goods could be exported by floating them downstream, the journey upstream was very long and difficult. Boatmen had to fight the current by using poles and ropes. The trip upriver from New Orleans to Cincinnati took months. The fastest known time was 78 days.

On the other hand, importing manufactures from the East was far too costly because the goods first had to be carted across the mountains and then shipped down the Ohio.

Because of this, the settlers west of the mountains had to do without many commonplace items that were regarded as necessities in the older parts of the country. Life was hard, and only the most daring and ambitious were willing to settle there.

But the steamboat changed all that. Shortly after steamboats appeared on the Ohio River in 1811, the river towns boomed. Steamboats had the power to go upstream. They could make the trip from New Orleans up to Cincinnati in 25 days instead of 78. Goods could now be brought into the river towns at prices low enough for everyone to afford. As trade flourished and settlers swarmed to the area, Cincinnati and St. Louis grew from towns into cities—the first real cities west of the Appalachians. Cincinnati began building its own steamboats and steam engines. Foundries, forges and machine shops sprang up as part of the new industry, and soon Cincinnati became a machinery manufacturing center.

With trade and industry booming, Cincinnati became the first major inland rival of the Eastern seaboard cities.

St. Louis, further westward, grew more slowly. It was the "gateway to the West," a place where travelers stopped to pick up supplies before pushing on ahead. Each week, Mississippi river boats brought dozens of families into St. Louis from the East or the South. Many of them continued on, but others stayed to settle the land.

St. Louis was also a fur-processing center, and the main market and supply center for the farmers of the surrounding countryside.

St. Louis' growth continued to lag behind that of Cincinnati. In 1840, when Cincinnati had 46,000 inhabitants, St. Louis only had about 17,000.

But with the discovery of gold in California in 1848, adventurers and prospectors from all over the country flocked to the west coast. They congregated in St. Louis to collect the equipment and supplies they needed for the remainder of the journey. Steamboats filled with men and supplies were lined up 20 deep at St. Louis' docks.

By 1850, the city's population had grown to 77,000, a gain of 60,000 in 10 years. During the next decade, trade continued to increase, and by 1854 St. Louis had outstripped Cincinnati as a center of river trade. By 1860, its population was 160,000.

Many people in both cities grew rich, and they spent their money on the luxuries and comforts that were imported from the East. They lived and dressed ostentatiously, trying to duplicate the sophistication of New York, Boston and Philadelphia.

But they had their own cultural distinctions that set them apart from the Eastern seaports. So many German immigrants had settled in Cincinnati that by 1850 the city had a very German flavor. German customs were widespread, German dishes were popular in almost every kitchen, German-style beer gardens sprang up everywhere and German music was heard and sung frequently. The public schools even offered courses in German.

Theaters, libraries, art galleries and concert halls flourished in both cities as people turned their attention to the intellectual and cultural sides of life. By the second half of the 19th century, neither Cincinnati nor St. Louis bore any resemblance to frontier towns. They were both established cities, the commercial and cultural hubs of America's heartland. The frontier had passed them by.

To the south of these cities, near the mouth of the Mississippi River, lay New Orleans. When Cincinnati and St. Louis were still only frontier outposts, New Orleans was already a thriving, bustling port city.

Located just 100 miles up the Mississippi River from the Gulf of Mexico, New Orleans was a seaport as well as a river port. Oceangoing vessels came into its harbor through the Gulf, while riverboats carried produce down from the farms and villages stretching along the Mississippi.

With such an excellent location, New Orleans' future seemed unlimited. Many people thought that one day it would become the greatest port in the world.

In its early years, New Orleans had been ruled first by the French, then by the Spanish, then again by the French. In 1803, Napoleon sold it to the United States along with the rest of the Louisiana Territory.

But the people, who were called Creoles, could not regard themselves as Americans for many generations. They had their own legal codes and customs, and were unfamiliar with the English common law that was practiced in America. They spoke mainly French, and had their own distinctive food and clothing, their own French opera and their own special carnival, called the Mardi Gras. Their entire culture was different from that of the rest of the United States.

The Creole aristocracy looked down upon the rough-mannered Yankee traders who poured into their city from the Mississippi riverboats. They felt much more comfortable with the European merchants and seamen who came from across the ocean.

New Orleans was a very gay and cosmopolitan city that attracted adventurers, pirates and thieves from all over the world. Gambling, drinking, smuggling and prostitution were part of everyday life.

The coming of the steamboat made river trade more profitable for New Orleans than it had been before, and the city grew at a dizzying pace. But the Creoles were much more easygoing than Yankee merchants and businessmen. While other cities were doing all they could to secure more trade for themselves, New Orleans merchants were content to let things drift along at a leisurely pace.

No warehouses were built along the docks to store goods. Perishables were left out on the open wharves in all sorts of weather, so that all too often produce just rotted. In one season, $100,000 worth of tobacco went bad on the docks. Flour and pork often got moldy. There was no central market place and no auction house. Streets were unpaved until well into the 19th century, except in the "American quarter," where cobblestones were put down in 1817.

Because of this neglect, other ports were able to steal trade away from New Orleans. In 1825, New York built a canal across the width of the state to Lake Erie. The "big ditch," as the Erie Canal was called, was a tremendous success.

Farmers of the northern Ohio country could ship their goods directly to New York City at very low rates, instead of sending them down the Ohio and Mississippi Rivers to New Orleans. The canal made New York the leading port in the nation. Hard-driving, ambitious merchants and bankers also contrived to lure much of the Southern cotton trade into New York, so that by 1850 New York was exporting more cotton than New Orleans.

New Orleans' languor probably stemmed more from its climate than from its cultural heritage. The weather was hot and humid enough to wilt anyone's energies, and the surrounding swamps and bayous bred mosquitoes carrying deadly yellow fever and malaria. Cholera, too, was common, so that the death rate was always high in the city.

New Orleans probably reached its commercial peak during the 1830s. But Northern states, in imitation of New York, were building canals that siphoned more river traffic away from New Orleans, so the city gradually declined. The Civil War and the chaos of the reconstruction years wiped out its prosperity altogether.

Even without the war, it is unlikely that New Orleans would have regained its former stature. Its fortunes depended heavily on river trade, and by the middle of the 19th century a rival form of transportation had emerged—the railroad.

The first serious attempt to build a commercial railroad was made by the city of Baltimore. Businessmen and bankers there had enviously eyed New York's success with the Erie Canal and wanted to capture some of the Ohio Valley trade for themselves. In 1828 they came up with a plan for laying iron tracks over the mountains and into the Ohio Valley as the foundation for a Baltimore and Ohio Railroad. By 1830, a double track had been laid from Baltimore to Ellicotts' Mills, 13 miles away.

The original idea was to use horse-drawn railroad cars, since steam locomotives were still little more than inventors' playthings.

But while the tracks were being laid, an inventor named Peter Cooper built a tiny steam locomotive that he called "Tom Thumb." It was able to puff along on tracks at about four miles an hour.

Stagecoach owners, who were threatened by the appearance of a steam-powered vehicle, challenged the "Tom Thumb" to a race.

The small locomotive and a horse-drawn car were placed side by side on double tracks. The horse took an early lead, but "Tom Thumb" soon caught up and passed it. Then, just near the finish, "Tom Thumb" broke down—a victim of mechanical failure.

The horse won, but its supremacy was short-lived. Better steam locomotives were built, and soon they were hauling tons of freight into Baltimore. By 1850 the iron tracks reached the Ohio Valley, and by 1858 the first B&O train rolled into Cincinnati.

Afraid of being outdone, other Eastern cities followed Baltimore's lead. New York, despite its new canal, began building a railroad, too. Pittsburgh and Philadelphia joined forces to get the Pennsylvania railroad started. Massachusetts undertook a Boston-to-Albany railroad.

The new railroads branched out rapidly. They had been born in the banks and business offices of the large Eastern cities, but as they pushed westward they, in turn, created new towns and cities along their routes.

The more ambitious and farsighted cities of the interior tried to attract as many railroads as possible, for it was becoming clear that without good rail connections their trade would suffer.

New Orleans, too far south to be included in the first

wave of railroad building, lost still more trade to her Northern rivals.

In contrast to New Orleans was a village that owed its spectacular rise to the railroads. This was Chicago, a swampy, bad-smelling town on Lake Michigan.

Chicago had the most phenomenal growth of any city in the United States. Between 1830 and 1930 it grew from a settlement of 50 people to a metropolis of three and one-third million.

Its early growth rested on a wave of land speculation touched off by a plan to build a canal through the town that would link Lake Michigan with the Mississippi. Everyone wanted to get in on the venture, and land prices boomed. In 1836, a Chicago newspaper revealed that land had "risen in value at the rate of 100% per day."

The lure of enormous profits attracted some of the most ambitious and energetic men in the country to Chicago. Financiers, real estate speculators, lawyers, businessmen and merchants all poured into the town. Along with them came the swindlers, crooks and gamblers, also looking for quick profits.

The collapse came in 1837. Land values dropped from more than $10 million to a low of about $1¼ million. Hundreds were ruined. Work on the canal stopped for lack of funds.

Many Chicagoans headed further west, but others stayed behind to start over again. They found a livelihood in providing goods for westward-bound travelers, since Chicago was the last stopping-off point before the empty prairie. In addition, the farmland surrounding Chicago began to produce a surplus of grain which could be shipped east on Lake Michigan.

Restless businessmen wanted to build a railroad that would bring more grain in from the countryside, but the big

bankers in the East were not interested. Chicagoans decided
to finance it themselves by selling stock in very small lots.
People responded eagerly, even though most could only afford two or three shares. Enough money was raised this way
to finance a railroad.

By 1848, 10 miles of track had been laid, and carloads of
wheat were rolling into Chicago. The railroad earned $2,000
a month during its first year of business. Chicago was on its
way to becoming the railroad center of America.

Just seven years later, Chicago had 10 trunk lines and 11
branch lines. The train whistle was a common sound as 96
trains a day chugged in and out of the city. Much conniving
and many shady deals lay behind Chicago's success in attracting railroads. Fortunes were made overnight, and the city
pulsed with more energy and exuberance than any other place
in America. It was a brash, flamboyant city that aroused
fierce loyalty and pride in its own citizens, while sparking the
envy of other cities.

New towns and cities continued to spring up in areas that
were opened by railroads, steamboats and canals. Manufacturing boomed as businessmen raced to produce more goods
for the growing Western markets. Heavy industry was born
out of the urgent need to produce steamboat engines, iron
rails and locomotives. Iron ore had to be mined and proc-
essed, creating a giant iron industry in Pennsylvania. Iron
processing depended on an abundance of coal, so coal mining
became another big industry.

The growth of industry turned towns and villages into
cities. By 1860, the urban population was one-fifth of the
total population. It had been only one-twentieth in 1790.

According to the census of 1860, there were nine American
cities with more than 100,000 population: Boston, New York,

Philadelphia, Baltimore, New Orleans, St. Louis, Cincinnati, Chicago and Brooklyn (considered a suburb of New York, even though it was actually a separate city then).

But for every large metropolis, there were hundreds of small towns and villages, mainly farming communities, where people had settled into a more simple life. The "typical American" was still a farmer or rural dweller, not a city person. He had little to do with factories, mines, overcrowded tenements, unemployment cycles or the vast complex of other city problems.

Between Chicago and the gold-rush city of San Francisco on the West Coast there was no place larger than Dubuque, Iowa, a town of 13,000. America still had plenty of growing room.

4

THE VANISHING
FRONTIER

Land! Just about anyone could get his own land here. That was the great promise of America.

There was so much empty land that people could get it "dirt cheap." In some areas it was actually free for anyone who promised to build a homestead on it. Impoverished immigrants, indentured servants and unskilled laborers could all get their own land and carve a better life for themselves out of the wilderness.

In Europe, land was costly, and people were bound by custom and economics to the same station in life as their forefathers. But America was different. Here, a person born in poverty was not doomed to remain poor all his life. With energy, ambition and hard work, he could settle his own land and be his own master. He might even become wealthy some day. The opportunity was there for all who had the courage to take it.

Land meant equality, too. In Europe, where class lines were rigidly drawn, a man was either born a "gentleman" or he was not. There was nothing he could do about it.

But in America, where everyone was a potential property

owner, class lines never became fixed. Although there were social distinctions based on wealth—particularly in the cities and in the South—it wasn't terribly hard for a man to climb the social ladder. All he needed was money.

On the frontier, especially, equality was the way of life. The harsh conditions of frontier living reduced everyone to the same level. It was man against nature—a life-or-death struggle that left no time for social refinements.

On the frontier, each family worked its own land without any hired help. There was no one to hire. No man would work another's land when there was so much good, cheap land all around. An abundance of land and a guarantee of equality and independence went hand in hand.

As the eastern part of the country filled up, restless, land-hungry Americans kept pushing further west into the wilderness.

Settlements turned into towns, and here and there a town grew into a city as the western migration continued. This march into the unknown followed a pattern that was described in Peck's *New Guide to the West*, published in Boston in 1837:

Generally, in all the western settlements, three classes, like the waves of the ocean, have rolled one after the other. First comes the pioneer, who depends for the subsistence of his family chiefly upon the natural growth of vegetation, called the "range," and the proceeds of hunting. . . . It is quite immaterial whether he ever becomes the owner of the soil. He is the occupant for the time being, pays no rent, and feels as independent as the "lord of the manor." With a horse, cow, and one or two breeders of swine, he strikes into the woods with his family, and becomes the founder of a new county, or perhaps state. He builds his cabin, gathers around him a few other families of similar tastes and habits, and occupies until the range is somewhat subdued, and hunting a little precarious, or, which is more frequently the case, till the neighbors crowd around, roads, bridges and fields annoy him, and he lacks elbow room. The preemption law enables him to dispose of his cabin and cornfield to the next class of emigrants; and, to employ his own figures, he "breaks for the high timber," "clears out for the New Purchase," or migrates to Arkansas or Texas to work the same process over.

The next class of emigrants purchase the lands, add field to field, clear out the roads, throw rough bridges over the streams, put up hewn log houses with glass windows and brick or stone chimneys, occasionally plant orchards, build mills, schoolhouses, court houses, etc., and exhibit the picture and forms of plain, frugal civilized life.

Another wave rolls on. The men of capitol and enterprise come. The settler is ready to sell out and take advantage of the rise in property, push further into the interior and become, himself, a man of capitol and enterprise in turn. The small village rises to a spacious town or city; substantial edifices of brick, extensive fields, orchards, gardens, colleges and churches are seen. Broadcloths, silks, leghorns, crapes, and all the refinements, luxuries, elegancies, frivolities and fashions are in vogue. Thus, wave after wave is rolling westward; the real Eldorado is still further on.

When the author wrote this in 1837, the "men of capitol and enterprise" had already come to large sections of Indiana, Illinois and Missouri. Further south, the "cotton kingdom" was also pushing west.

Planters in the deep South headed for new lands whenever their old fields got worn out from constant planting of cotton. They knew nothing about crop rotation to conserve the soil, and probably wouldn't have cared if they did know. There was always plenty of new land to move on to if the old soil went bad.

For this reason, Americans were notoriously bad farmers.

Their wasteful, careless methods shocked Europeans, who, out of necessity, tended their own lands very carefully.

By the 1820s, hundreds of "gone to Texas" farms dotted the South—worn out, abandoned cotton fields whose owners had headed west. A poor farmer and his family would make the journey in a wagon drawn by mules or oxen. A cow or two might be hitched to the back of the wagon, while the children walked alongside. When they reached frontier country where land was cheap, they often built "dog-run cabins" —two small cabins connected by a porch.

They planted corn and vegetables and, of course, cotton. If the land was particularly well suited to this crop, the farmer might become rich. But more often, the cotton grew fairly well for just a few years, and then the soil became worn out. Without a good cash crop there was no point in staying on the land. Then the family would pack up and move on again, to the virgin lands further west.

The rich plantation owners were migrating, too, although they moved their households in a more elegant style. The master and his family rode in a coach driven by a handsomely dressed driver, while the servants followed behind in wagons. Further on down the line were more wagons that held tools, furniture and supplies. Bringing up the rear were the men in charge of the livestock. They had to guide unruly herds of cattle, horses and hogs along the roads.

When the caravan reached the new plantation, homes were already waiting for them. Either a hired overseer or a member of the family had made the journey earlier to supervise the building of a new manor house and new cabins for the slaves.

In this way, the cotton planters of Virginia, Georgia and the Carolinas moved their culture and their way of life ever westward.

Onward they went, reaching Texas by the 1830s. Although the land belonged to Mexico, the Mexican government had permitted Americans to settle there. One pioneer, Stephen Austin, got permission to build a colony and recruit other American settlers. He was expected to bring in about 300 families, but he brought in thousands. Other Americans got land grants, and they, too, recruited pioneers.

By 1830, there were about 20,000 Americans in Texas, and the Mexican government was sorry it had ever let them in at all. The foreigners were murmuring about "independence," for they could not get along with the Mexican authorities. Finally, General Santa Anna led his Mexican Army into Texas to drive out the American settlers. Instead of fleeing, the Texans declared their independence. They adopted a constitution and hoisted the Lone Star Flag over their new republic.

The first big battle took place at a San Antonio mission called the Alamo. Less than 200 Texans tried to hold the Alamo against an army of several thousand Mexicans. On March 6, 1836, the battle was over. Every single Texan in the Alamo had been killed.

"Remember the Alamo" became the battle cry, as General Sam Houston pitched his Texas Army against Santa Anna's. The Mexican forces were trounced at the Battle of San Jacinto on April 21, 1836, and the war was over. Texas was free. Nine years later, the Lone Star Republic was admitted into the Union as a state.

Once Texas became part of the United States, Mexico felt even more threatened. There was no doubt that the Americans wanted to take over the rest of Mexico's southwest territories, including what are now the states of California and New Mexico.

Americans had been coming into these areas since the 1820s, when a trader named William Becknell first took his

wagons along a trail from Missouri to the Mexican village of
Santa Fe. This Santa Fe Trail became a famous trade route
into the Southwest, and from there American pioneers
branched out into California.

Now Americans wanted all these lands for themselves.
Thrilled with all they had accomplished and certain that their
causes were just, they felt it was their "manifest destiny to
occupy and possess the whole of the Continent which Providence has given us." So said the newspapers, and the young
poet Walt Whitman wrote that, in the interest of mankind,
America's "power and territory should be extended—the
further the better."

Americans felt they had a God-given right to all the land
from ocean to ocean, and in 1844 they elected a President
who would make sure they got it—James K. Polk.

Polk came into office on an expansionist platform, and by
May, 1846, America was at war with Mexico. After the American armies marched into Mexico, the war was over. In the
peace treaty of 1848, the United States got all the land north
of the Rio Grande River and west to the Pacific.

But this was not all the Americans wanted. They were expanding in the Northwest as well, and had narrowly missed
going to war with England over the Oregon Territory. The
two countries were supposed to share the territory, according
to a treaty signed in 1818. But the United States was claiming
all the land as far north as the parallel 54°40'.

Polk's campaign slogan had been "Fifty-four forty or fight,"
but once in office he decided it would be foolhardy to take on
England as well as Mexico. In 1846, England and the United
States signed a treaty setting the Oregon boundary line at the
49th parallel, as far as Puget Sound. This compromise ended
the threat of war and firmly established the boundary between the United States and western Canada.

Americans had been interested in Oregon since Lewis and

Clark first explored the area early in the 19th century. In 1810, John Jacob Astor set up a fur-trading post on the Columbia River, and in the 1820s the powerful Hudson's Bay Company took control of the Oregon fur trade. They made huge profits. In one year, a million dollars' worth of beaver skins and other furs were shipped to England from the Oregon trading post.

A small settlement grew up around the post, and the people branched out into other fields. They started catching and drying salmon, planted orchards, grew wheat and vegetables and built and ran a flour mill and a sawmill. Soon they were also exporting food.

In the 1830s, a number of missionaries headed out to the Pacific Northwest to teach the Christian religion to the Indians. They came along the Oregon Trail, an overland route through the Rocky Mountains that had been discovered by mountain fur trappers.

The missionaries built churches and schools in the Western wilderness, and it wasn't long before thousands of settlers had followed them across the Oregon Trail to the fertile valleys of the Pacific Coast.

Many of these settlers came all the way from the other side of the country, from New England and New York. Others came from the Mississippi Valley to escape the epidemics and fevers that were so common there.

By the 1840s, a steady stream of wagon trains was making the long journey to the Pacific Northwest. The "jumping off" point was Independence, Missouri, and some of the other nearby towns. Each spring, lines of covered wagons would begin the 2,000 mile trip across the plains and over the mountains. If they were lucky, they would reach Oregon before Thanksgiving.

The pioneers almost always traveled in large groups because of the great danger of Indian attacks. The open plains offered little protection, so every night the wagon trains pulled into a big circle. Each driver attached his wagon to the one in front, forming a fortlike ring of defense. Inside the ring, campfires were lit, women cooked dinner, children played and horses and cattle grazed. Sometimes there was singing and dancing well into the night. The men took turns at standing guard in the darkness, and even young boys were given guns and taught how to shoot.

The journey lasted about six months, and was filled with hardships. Sometimes wagons overturned and people lost all their possessions. The pioneers faced hunger, thirst and ill-ness, and a great many of them died along the way.

But those who made it settled into new, thriving farm communities. Towns and cities sprang up throughout Oregon; soon Seattle, on the shores of Puget Sound, became a major seaport.

Meanwhile, further south in California, the news flashed out—gold had been found!

On a clear morning in January, 1848, a man named James Marshall had been working at Sutter's Mill in the Sacramento Valley. "I shall never forget that morning," he wrote. "As I was taking my usual walk . . . my eye was caught by a glimpse of something shining in the bottom of the ditch. . . . I reached my hand down and picked it up. It made my heart thump, for I was certain it was gold. . . . I sat down and began to think right hard. . . . In a very short time, we discovered that the whole country was but one bed of gold. So there, stranger, is the entire history of the gold discovery in California. . . ."

Within a year, hordes of prospectors poured into California from all over the country. The "forty-niners" came with little more than their picks and shovels, and their pans for washing gold out of the sand and gravel. They started mining towns with names like Hangtown, Skunk Gulch and Git-up-and-Git.

San Francisco, the main port of entry, became a wild chaotic town. Its streets and taverns were overflowing with adventurers, speculators, swindlers, drifters, prostitutes and other such types who populate a "boom town." Prices were wildly inflated, with eggs costing a dollar apiece. Rents were insane—a cot under a tent might cost $20 a week. By 1851, the village of San Francisco had become a full-grown city, jammed with more than 20,000 people.

However, in just a few years, there was hardly any gold left in California. The mining towns turned into empty ghost towns, and people settled into other occupations, particularly farming.

By the end of the 1850s, America owned the land from one ocean to another. Well over half of it was already settled, but there were vast, empty gaps. Most of the people lived between the East Coast and the Mississippi River. The rest lived mainly along the Pacific coast and in Texas.

The pattern of heavy settlement had skipped right over the vast plains and prairies west of the Mississippi. People preferred to brave the dangers of the Oregon Trail rather than settle on the flat, dry, treeless plains that stretched on forever.

The pioneers were used to wooded areas, and they didn't know what to do with the thick prairie sod, where grass grew as tall as a man. With so few trees they wouldn't have enough wood to build their homes. What's more, the flatness of the land would leave them wide open to Indian raids.

So the sprawling Western plains remained only sparsely settled while the Pacific coast was filling up. There were no really large cities between Chicago and San Francisco, and the railroads only went as far west as Chicago and St. Louis. There wasn't enough population further on to support a railroad.

But people along the Pacific Coast began pressing for a transcontinental railroad that would link them directly with the population centers of the East. In 1862, Congress allotted funds and land to two railroad companies, and work was begun on America's first cross-country railroad.

The Union Pacific Railroad started building a line westward from Omaha, Nebraska, which was also to be linked by rail to Chicago.

The other company, the Central Pacific, began its railroad line in Sacramento, California, and worked eastward. The two lines were supposed to join up somewhere in between.

The men working on this project had to be good riflemen as well as strong laborers. They kept their guns close at hand, for at times they had to drop their tools to fight off Indian attacks. The crew that was heading west was made up mainly of Irish laborers who came from the large Eastern cities. The workers starting from Sacramento were mainly Chinese and Mexican.

As the two lines of track came closer together, strong rivalry sprang up between the two crews. They each wanted to claim the credit for having laid the most track. Every day they checked by telegraph to see how much mileage the other group had covered.

On May 10, 1869, East and West were finally united. Government officials and other dignitaries from the East boarded a train at Omaha and rode west over the new tracks. At the same time, dignitaries from the West Coast got on a train at Sacramento and headed east. They met at Promontory Point in Utah, where the last bit of work was still to be done.

Gentlemen in high silk hats stood shoulder to shoulder with roughly clad Irish, Chinese and Mexican laborers to watch while the last tie was put down. Then spikes of silver and other metals were driven into place. The last spike, made of pure gold, was a gift from the state of California.

As soon as the golden spike was hammered in, a tumultuous roar arose from the crowd. The two engines, which had been facing each other across the last section of track, moved together slowly until they touched.

Telegraphs tapped out the news to the rest of the country, and every town and city celebrated the historic event. Americans had advanced all the way across a continent and linked their two oceans by rail—and most of it happened in the 80 years since George Washington became the country's first president.

The railroad helped unite the country spiritually as well as geographically. America didn't start out as a unit. It was 13 separate colonies, with many regional differences. In a very short time it mushroomed into a big, sprawling country with even more diversity. The people were not homogenous. They didn't have common origins or a common religion. They didn't have a common culture, and many of them hardly spoke the language. It would not have been too surprising if they had splintered off into separate regional groups, as almost happened during the Civil War.

But the rapid growth of railroads, steamboats, canals and turnpikes helped draw the country closer together by providing quick, easy access from one region to another. People became linked through trade and business, and they shared pride in having conquered a vast wilderness in less than a century.

The new transcontinental railroad speeded the development of the remaining frontier areas. Shortly after East and West were joined, the Union Pacific Railroad began promoting settlement in the Western plains and prairies. The railroad owned a lot of land in Nebraska, Colorado, Wyoming and Utah, which it was selling cheaply. Groups of settlers who bought these lands could travel out west on the Union Pacific at reduced rates.

The federal government was also encouraging settlement. In 1862, Congress had passed the Homestead Act, under which the head of a family could receive 160 acres of public land free. All he had to do was swear that he and his family would live on that land and cultivate it for the next five years.

Many immigrants and poor farmers from the East took advantage of these offers, particularly after the Panic of 1873, when so many people lost whatever they had.

Typical of these settlers was the family of young Mont Hawthorne. Mont had been born in Pennsylvania in 1865. When he was five years old, his family moved to Virginia. In recalling these years, he wrote:

"Pickings was slim enough our first year down South; they was slimmer the second; come spring the third year everything had gone to rick and ruin. The drought had got our tobacco during the second summer so we was short of money to lay in our bought provisions and we hadn't raised near enough to last us over."

When a fire wiped out what little they had, Mont's father decided it was time to move on. With no money, the only thing they could do was file a claim for free land in Nebraska under the Homestead Act.

"It took the hard times of '73 to settle the plains," said Mont. "Just like with us, free land or anything else free looked good."

The railroad took them into Nebraska, but they had to travel another 60 miles by wagon and on foot to reach their piece of land.

After several days of exhausting travel in freezing weather and snowstorms, they finally arrived at the site. "The girls and me just looked at each other," Mont wrote. "Why there wasn't a thing to be seen around there but snow, and a clump of cottonwoods off a piece to the right, and we was all of a half mile from the Middle Loup River.

". . . [Father] dropped down on his knees to scrape the snow away, then he come up with a double handful of rich soil. Mama pulled off her gloves and squeezed some of it between her fingers. After a minute, she looked up, smiled, and says, 'Yes, Sam, this is a lot better than we had back in Virginia.'"

During the first year on the prairie, the family built their house, planted a little garden and lots of sod corn and plowed the ground to get it ready for the next year. It took a full year for the thick prairie sod to be shaped up for planting.

There were only five other families in their lonely valley. They were so vulnerable to Indian attacks that they had to build a stockade to take refuge in whenever the Sioux rode out of the Black Hills.

In this way, frontier life constantly repeated itself. The Nebraska settlers of the 1870s lived in much the same way as Daniel Boone and his Kentucky pioneers a hundred years earlier. Although most of the pioneers in the Middle and Far West had emigrated from other countries—Germany, Sweden, Norway, etc.—frontier life carved them into similar molds. They all had to be hardy, resourceful, industrious and self-reliant just to survive under primitive frontier conditions. They depended on their guns for both food and protection, and a man always kept his rifle at his side. Even today, it is very hard to pass laws designed to separate Americans from their guns.

The pioneers learned to use whatever they had at hand, and to invent new ways of doing things to cope with new conditions. Necessity shaped their character and gave them traits that were distinctly American, born out of the unique American experience of frontier living.

Of course, frontier life differed in detail, depending on the region. While the Kentucky pioneers had lived in log cabins, a prairie family built a "soddy"—a small house made of the thick prairie top soil. Trees were scarce on the prairie, so people turned to the only building material available.

Sod houses were snug and warm in winter, and cool in summer. But they were awful when it rained. Mont Hawthorne recalled: "Lots of times folks had to move outside after a big rain because when it quit raining outside, it begun raining inside. Why a sod roof could turn out to be just like having a bunch of little springs in the ceiling, with dirty water running down into the food and wetting up the bedding. Then if the rain kept up, big chunks of mud would start to fall, and unless a sod house was built with real good rafters that was strong enough to hold up the weight of all that wet dirt, the roof would cave in."

Somehow, the prairie settlers managed to survive their soddies, and the Western lands grew more populated.

By 1890, the federal census report included the following statement: "Up to and including 1880 the country had a frontier of settlement, but at present the unsettled area has been so broken into by isolated bodies of settlement that there can hardly be said to be a frontier line."

America's frontier had vanished.

The empty lands that had seemed so inexhaustible were now dotted with farms and villages and towns. Although there was still plenty of room for growth, the best lands had already been taken. This meant that America was no longer a place of unbounded growth and opportunity for all. Certain limits had been reached, and a very significant chapter in American history had come to a close.

5

THE MACHINE AGE COMES TO RURAL AMERICA

The whole Thompson family was out working in the fields, trying to harvest their wheat crop in time. They had only a few days to do the job because soon the fine ripe grain would break and rot.

The family worked throughout the day and late into the night, cutting the wheat by hand with cradle scythes and then tying the cut stalks together in big bunches. It was exhausting work, and even though all seven members of the family kept at it steadily, it was still very slow.

Their neighbors couldn't help. They were having the same trouble harvesting their own wheat crops. Some of the luckier ones had been able to hire a few workers to help with the job, but farm labor was very scarce in Illinois in the 1840s. What's more, most farmers couldn't afford to hire anyone.

The Thompson family worked almost around the clock for the next few days. Finally, one bright, hot morning, Mr. Thompson looked out across the remaining acres of wheat and announced, "That's it. The grain's broke. Might as well turn the hogs loose in there now. We just planted too much."

So the hogs feasted on several acres of ruined wheat that

the family wasn't able to harvest in time. Their farm was in one of the most fertile grain-growing areas in all of America, but that wasn't much help to them. What good was it if the virgin prairie soil yielded large crops when they couldn't harvest it all?

They had planted a lot because wheat prices were getting higher every day. More and more people were coming into Illinois and the surrounding areas, and more food was needed to supply the growing towns.

But farmers were still using many of the old methods and simple tools that their ancestors had used centuries ago. They clung to these ancient practices as if they were part of their religion, and it was very hard to convince them to try new techniques. For example, for many years following the invention of the iron plow, farmers kept right on using their old wooden ones. They believed iron would "poison the soil" or make more weeds grow. The demand for iron plows didn't really take hold until about 1815.

Because of such superstitions and habits, farmers in the early 19th century were producing only a very small surplus. Nine farm people could only raise enough to feed themselves plus one city person. This meant that the vast majority of people had to work on farms in order to supply enough food for the nation.

Mr. Thompson's crop had been especially large in 1843 because he had started using a new kind of plow—a steel plow invented six years earlier by a blacksmith named John Deere. Mr. Thompson and his neighbors had been working with iron plows before, but it was very hard to use them on the tough prairie sod. The thick black soil stuck to the iron plows so that they couldn't work properly. This made plowing very slow and difficult, and farmers on the prairie couldn't cultivate all their lands.

Necessity—and the lure of rising food prices—led them to try Deere's steel plow. It worked beautifully on the sticky Illinois soil, and the blades stayed clean. This allowed the farmers to cultivate more land and grow larger crops. But the problem of harvesting them still remained.

It wasn't until several years later that Mr. Thompson heard of another new invention—a reaper that could cut 15 or more acres of grain in a single day. It had been invented by an Easterner named Cyrus McCormick.

Actually, McCormick had first built a reaper back in 1831, but it was a clumsy, imperfect machine that was so noisy it frightened the horses that had to pull it. During the next 13 years, McCormick kept improving his reaper, but the farmers of his native Virginia were still very slow to accept it.

McCormick put on demonstrations of the machine throughout the state, sometimes successfully and sometimes not. His failures made the farmers skeptical about this "new fangled" device.

According to one story, McCormick was demonstrating his reaper one day on a rough, hilly farm in Lexington, Virginia. A hundred people were watching as the reaper clattered and shook violently while cutting the wheat. Finally, the farmer couldn't stand it anymore.

"Stop that thing!" he shouted. "It's rattling the heads off my wheat!"

People in the crowd started laughing, and some even poked fun at McCormick. The dejected young inventor was about to take his equipment and leave when a neighboring farmer invited him onto his own fields.

"I'll give you a chance," he said. "See if you can cut my wheat."

His fields were flat and smooth, with hardly any stones on them at all. The reaper performed beautifully, cutting six acres of wheat in a remarkably short time. The spectators were so impressed that they formed a procession and drove the reaper to the public square in Lexington for all to see.

However, other failures followed, for the reaper really could not work well on rocky, uneven ground. By 1844, Mc-Cormick decided to head west with his invention. He was sure his reaper would work perfectly on the endless acres of flat, stone-free prairie soil.

He set out with $300 in his pocket, and for the next two years he traveled throughout the vast prairie lands trying to interest farmers in his machines. The prairie farmers, who were growing more grain than they could possibly harvest with their ancient scythes, were ready to try something new.

But there was a problem. The reapers cost $100 each, and very few farmers had that much money. They didn't produce enough of a surplus to acquire much cash, and it would have taken most of them several years to save up enough to buy a reaper.

McCormick's faith in his invention—and in the basic honesty of farmers—was so great that he decided to try something no one had done before. He decided to sell his reapers on credit; farmers wouldn't have to pay for them until after they had sold their grain. The reaper would allow them to harvest such large crops that a machine could pay for itself in one season.

This was an offer that farmers couldn't resist, and orders started pouring in. McCormick had been licensing other manufacturers to produce reapers for him, but now he decided to settle down and start his own factory.

He wanted a site with good transport facilities so that he could ship his machines throughout the Midwest. Also, he needed to find financial backers and workers for his factory.

His instincts led him to Chicago, because he felt that

eventually the wealth of the Midwest was going to concentrate there. Even though at that time Chicago was still only a swampy little town on Lake Michigan, the businessmen there were boldly adventurous, always eager to try new money-making schemes. Furthermore, they were trying to promote the town as a railroad center, and McCormick was sure they would succeed.

He guessed right. The inventor found everything he was looking for in Chicago—financial backers, an abundance of labor and, in just a few years, more railroad connections than he could have hoped for. McCormick's reaper factory and Chicago grew up together, each helping the other get larger. As Chicago went from a small town to a city of millions, McCormick's factory mushroomed into the giant International Harvester Company, the largest producer of farm machinery in the world.

Small farmers like Mr. Thompson and his neighbors bought reapers on credit, and most were able to pay off their debt after the first or second harvest.

This credit buying worked well, setting the pattern for the years ahead, when billions of dollars' worth of merchandise would be sold on "buy now, pay later" plans.

Other new farm inventions sprang up about this time, too, and all of them enabled the farmer to grow more with less effort. Ancient farming methods that had been in use for centuries were swept aside as farmers were caught in the grip of an agricultural revolution.

No longer did farmers walk their fields with sacks of seed slung over their shoulder, scattering handfuls at a time. Seeding could be done far more quickly and efficiently by mechanical drills, which put the seeds exactly the right distance into the ground. By 1860, farmers who were using the drills needed only two bushels of seed for every three needed in the hand-sown method. What's more, the drills had increased their yield by six to eight bushels per acre.

The old threshing process, in which the grain was separated from the straw by putting it on a platform and having horses tramp on it over and over again, was discarded in favor of a portable thresher that ran on steam power.

These new threshers were very large and much too expensive for a farmer to buy himself. They were owned and operated as a traveling business. Each machine was run by a crew of five or six men. They would start working in Texas, where the wheat ripened first, and go from farm to farm with their thresher, gradually working their way up north.

The steam-powered thresher, the reaper, the mechanical seeder and the many other 19th-century farming inventions were just a prelude to what would come in the 20th century, when agriculture became almost totally mechanized. Today, huge diesel-powered "combines" zoom across enormous fields, reaping and threshing as they go, so that the clean grain falls into a sack only seconds after the stalks are cut.

The process of farm mechanization that began around the middle of the 19th century progressed rapidly in the next 50 years. Better varieties of seed and fertilizer were discovered, and farmers were learning the benefits of proper crop rotation.

All these discoveries enabled farmers to bring many more acres of land under cultivation without hiring additional workers. It changed their lives in other ways, too. Sons were able to attend school for a longer time because they weren't needed so much on the family farm. Machines could do the work of several men, thereby freeing children for other pursuits.

Large crop surpluses gave the farmer cash to buy goods that were previously made at home or that the family had done without. They could get shoes or soap from a store instead of making such things themselves. Even though the farmer's wife still made most of the family's clothes, she could treat herself to a popular new device called a sewing machine. Like McCormick's reaper, this invention was also being sold on the installment plan. Its chief promoter was Isaac Merrit Singer, founder of the Singer Sewing Machine Company.

Thus, the mechanization of agriculture lightened the work load of everyone on a farm, including the farmer's wife and children.

Successful and ambitious farmers were able to enlarge their farms, mechanize their operations still more and greatly increase their yield per acre.

But, for every farmer who broke with tradition and staked his future on the new inventions and techniques, others just drifted along in the same old way. Their farms remained small; their methods were inefficient, and they had only very small surpluses or no surplus at all.

As farm mechanization increased, these small farmers couldn't compete with the more sophisticated operators. They were constantly in debt, and when hard times came, many of them lost their land. The small farms were swallowed up by the large farms, which became even larger. This cycle was just starting at the end of the 19th century, and it accelerated as the 20th century wore on.

Sometimes the small farmers went under because of economic depressions or recessions; at other times they simply couldn't get back on their feet after a natural disaster such as a prolonged drought or an insect plague. Entire harvests or herds of livestock could be wiped out by disease. Crops could fail because of too much rain or too little rain. Very strong winds could flatten a whole cornfield. The frost could come too soon.

Bigger farmers were able to withstand these crises better than the small farmers. Their mechanized operations usually gave them a cash reserve to fall back on, so they had the means to start over again.

As the 20th century dawned, a trend became apparent. Farms were getting larger and more mechanized. There were fewer small farms than there had been in the previous century and—most significant—there were less people actually engaged in agriculture. The rural population as a whole was still growing, but the growth was in the rural towns and villages rather than on the farms.

People were leaving the land and heading for the big cities. The sons and daughters of farmers, better educated than their parents, were increasingly attracted by the opportunities and variety of city life. The urban population was growing at six times the rural rate.

6

"GIVE ME YOUR TIRED, YOUR POOR . . ."

At the same time that new inventions were reducing the number of people needed on the farms, other forces were at work swelling the urban centers. Immigrants were pouring into the country at an astonishing rate. The years between 1890 and 1914 saw the greatest wave of immigration in American history. Fifteen million foreign-born people came to settle on these shores during this 24-year period—matching the entire total of immigrants who had come to America during the 75 years before 1890.

These new immigrants were different from the old in that most of them came from the poor countries of southern and eastern Europe. Also, they clustered in the cities and industrial centers rather than spreading out on the land.

This was partly because America no longer had a frontier, so that land was not as cheap as it had been. It was also partly because more money was needed for equipment. The new machinery that made farming profitable cost a lot of money, far more than most of these very poor immigrants could afford.

But also, and possibly most important, they came to the

cities because they had lost faith in the land. In their own countries, farming had only brought them poverty and hardship. Many were peasants who had to labor in the fields day after day, only to turn over most of their harvest to the landlord and the Church. Those who owned their own land were often not much better off. Their plots were so small and the yields so meager that they could barely feed themselves. They lived an uncertain existence, always at the mercy of nature and always fearful that next year might bring famine. To make matters worse, these peasants and small farmers were mired at the bottom of the social scale in class-conscious Europe, scorned and exploited by the gentry and merchants.

America beckoned to them, offering them jobs as unskilled workers in factories and mines, and on the enormous construction projects that were forging a powerful nation. Workers were needed to build the railroads, bridges, canals and highways that linked the country together. Labor was in heavy demand in America, so that wages were higher than in Europe. American industrialists and builders actively recruited immigrant workers, often supplying their passage money so they could make the trip.

Thus, the last great wave of immigrants came with the intention of changing their whole way of life. They were leaving their native countries in the hope of finding a better life in the urban-industrial centers of America.

Earlier immigrants had come with other goals in mind. The first wave began around 1815, at the close of the Napoleonic Wars. They were mainly small farmers from England, Scotland, Ireland, Wales, Germany and the Scandinavian countries. For the most part, they were seeking good, cheap land. Many of them came with sufficient funds to buy a few acres and settle down quickly, so they didn't linger in the cities very long. Others needed jobs first in order to save up enough from their wages to buy some property.

Farming was their goal, and they had come because they felt it was better to be a farmer in America than in their own countries. In England, being a farmer often meant being a tenant on the estate of some lord, paying high rents, tithes and taxes and generally holding a low station in life. But in America, a farmer was a landowner who paid no rent, no tithes and few taxes. He was a respected member of society who didn't have to bow before any lord since all were equal.

Those hardy, adventurous souls who came first sent letters back home urging relatives and friends to follow. They praised the virtues of their new land so that America seemed like a paradise where everyone was comfortable and well-fed.

This steady stream of letters aroused great excitement back in the immigrants' native towns and villages. When someone in a town received a letter from America, it would be passed from person to person until everyone knew all that was in it. Other letters were printed in newspapers or periodicals, so that their effect was even more widespread.

The letters inspired thousands to try their luck in this new land, and although some were disappointed to find that America was not all they had been led to believe, most were pleased. They in turn sent letters back home overflowing with praise of their new country, and the cycle continued.

Such letters played a strategic role in attracting immigrants to America. Although they were often filled with exaggerations of America's wealth, many of them stressed a common theme: that if a man was willing to work hard in this new country he could have a good life and plenty to eat. But letter after letter warned that America was no place for the lazy.

As one Welsh immigrant in Missouri wrote, "Let no one

think that he will emigrate and not have to work. If so, poverty is certain to overtake him. You need to work as hard here as in any part of the world but elsewhere it is to pay taxes whereas here it buys a farm."

Not only did people have to work hard, but they also had to work at top speed. Immigrants were surprised to find that Americans did everything at a very fast pace, as if there were not enough time in the world for all they wanted to accomplish. In order to keep up, the immigrants had to learn to work much faster than was customary in Europe. Despite this, their enthusiasm remained high, and they wrote of their new country in glowing terms.

The spirit of many of the letters was typified by this account from another Welsh immigrant to his parents, brothers and sisters:

I am sure that there is no more fertile land in creation than in the state of Iowa. It produces its crops without the need of manure. It contains from 5 to 20 feet of rich black earth. It is easy to farm. One can see miles of it as flat as a board without a single stone near it. After plowing it once it is like a garden and they can raise anything on it. . . .

I have taken 320 acres and have paid for 240 of them and I must pay for the remainder within a year. I have talked with men who have been here three or four years and they had but little or nothing to start with and now some of them are worth their thousands of dollars. . . .

You urge me to come back to the Old Country but there is no liklihood of my doing that very soon as my adopted country is better than the land of my birth and if only you had had the heart to come here 20 years ago you would have seen and proved the excellence of the country and we would have been parents and children together. I prefer to say like the Yankees and in their language too:

Come along, come along, make no delay,
Come from every nation and come from every way,
Our lands they are broad enough, don't feel alarm
For Uncle Sam is rich enough to give us all a farm.

Of course, not all of the earlier immigrants were farmers.
Many were craftsmen, artisans, mechanics or miners who
were attracted by the higher wages and better working conditions in America. However, many of these immigrants were
not as enthusiastic about their new country as farmers.

For one thing, they found that conditions were very unstable. Sometimes there was an abundance of jobs; sometimes there was hardly any work to be had. An immigrant
couldn't be certain that his particular skill would be in demand at the time he arrived or in the area in which he
planned to settle. For the unskilled, things were even more
uncertain.

As one Pennsylvania coal miner wrote:

I know that this country is better than the old for raising a
family and that the children of workingmen have better advantages for education and through this to become famous; but
although these advantages are to be had in America, the head of
the family has to get work before these blessings can be enjoyed.
Every man with a little common sense knows that it is a serious
thing to bring a family to a foreign country with just enough
money to reach land . . . and by the time he gets there, failing to
get work. We know of some in such trouble and it is very likely
that we shall see others again before the end of the summer. I
hope that these lines will help to prevent my dear countrymen
from falling into such worries and troubles.

Since farmers could feel more certain of a good livelihood
in America than workers, they formed the majority of the
immigrant population in the first half of the 19th century.

But the late 1840s saw the arrival of a new wave of immigrants who were too desperate to carefully weigh their prospects before coming to the New World. These were the Irish —and they came because they were starving.

The potato crop had failed in Ireland. Blight destroyed the entire crop in 1845 and then again in 1846. More than any other people of Europe, the Irish depended on the potato. It was the mainstay of their diet, and they fed it to their livestock as well. Without it they couldn't survive.

By 1847, thousands of Irish were dead of starvation. The countryside looked as if it had been struck by plague. Men, women and children were gaunt and haggard from hunger. Food was so scarce and prices so high that even a laborer with a steady job could afford no more than a little thin gruel every day for himself and his family—hardly enough to keep up their strength. It was a slow death. Everyone who depended on the farmer was starving too, including shopkeepers and merchants.

The death rate was staggering. In some rural districts half the population died of starvation. Almost no livestock was left. The entire countryside was devastated.

Facing hunger and death, the Irish fled their native land. They sold everything they owned for passage money, and boarded ships bound for the United States and Canada.

Unlike most previous immigrants, they had no food to take along with them for the long voyage, and had to depend on the notoriously foul-tasting, scanty meals provided by the ships. Ship owners made a large profit from these unfortunate Irish immigrants, sometimes jamming twice the legal number into small, damp, bad-smelling and unsanitary steerage quarters. Thousands never reached the New World because disease or starvation claimed them first.

Food and sanitary conditions were somewhat better on American ships than on those heading for Canada. Out of

100,000 Irish who fled to Canada in one year, 6,100 died aboard ship and another 4,100 died shortly after their arrival. Those who survived found conditions in Canada so bad that many of them left at once for the United States.

During the next decade, hundreds of thousands of ragged, hungry Irish immigrants poured into the northeastern part of the country. For the most part they stayed there, crowding into the slums of the large urban centers and the factory towns. They took whatever work they could find. Men worked as low-paid laborers in mills, mines and construction projects, while women became maids and scrubwomen.

Although they had come mainly from the rural areas of Ireland, they wanted nothing to do with farming now. Famine had scarred their minds and bodies, and they no longer trusted the land. Thus, the great majority of the Irish concentrated in the cities, particularly in Boston and New York, where large Irish-American communities already existed.

Germans were also coming to America in large numbers at this time, for political as well as economic reasons. Many of the German immigrants were Catholic, just as the Irish were, so that their combined immigration greatly swelled the numbers of Catholics in America.

By tradition, America had always been open to all immigrants as a haven for the oppressed. The "open door" policy was part of the country's heritage, and most Americans were proud of it. But at the same time, antiforeign feeling also existed in the United States, and this grew stronger with the influx of so many Catholics.

The vast majority of Americans were Protestants whose attitude towards Catholics was somewhat less than friendly. The sudden, heavy Catholic immigration alarmed them and gave rise to a political party dubbed the Know-Nothings,

whose basic goal was to keep America for the Americans—
that is, for the native white Protestant population.

According to the party's doctrines, only native-born Americans should hold office, and immigrants should not be naturalized until they had lived here 21 years.

The party rose rapidly, and by 1854 it was a strong political force. However, it soon fell into a decline and faded out
entirely during the Civil War. But this was not the end of
anti-immigrant feelings by any means. It was only a fore-
shadowing of what was soon to come.

By the early 1860s, America's population had reached
about 31.5 million. Of these, more than four million were
foreign-born. Over 85 percent of the immigrants lived in the
Northern states of New York, Pennsylvania, Ohio, Illinois,
Wisconsin and Massachusetts.

In some of the large cities, such as New York, Cincinnati,
Chicago and Milwaukee, almost half the population was
foreign-born. Most of the immigrants had come from Ireland,
Germany, England, Scotland and Wales.

The newly arrived English, Scottish and Welsh were easily
assimilated into American society. This was natural enough,
since they came from the same stock as most native Americans. The Germans were not welcomed so readily, particularly the Catholics among them.

But most of the venom was reserved for the Irish, particularly in the old Puritan stronghold of Massachusetts.

The Anglo-Saxon New Englanders looked with contempt
upon the Celtic Irish, feeling that they were of inferior stock.
As long as the Irish "kept their place" and worked docilely as
servants or menial laborers, the native New Englanders were
not overly alarmed.

In Boston, particularly, the social lines were sharply drawn,
and the two groups remained completely separate. The divi-

sion even applied to such matters as public transportation. For example, in Cambridge there were two horse-drawn trolley cars that ran parallel to each other and were only a block apart. The native Bostonians used one line, and the Irish laborers and scrubwomen used the other. This was part of a strict social code, and it would have been unthinkable for an Irishman to board the "gentlemen's trolley" or for a maid to ride in the same car as her mistress.

More formal discrimination existed, too. In some establishments, particularly restaurants, signs were posted saying "No Dogs or Irish Allowed." Bigotry was also evident in the public schools. Recalling the attitude of the Yankee spinster "schoolmarms" in Lowell, Massachusetts, William Cardinal O'Connell said he "sensed the bitter antipathy, scarcely concealed, which nearly all these good women . . . felt toward those of us who had Catholic faith and Irish names. For any slight pretext we were severely punished. We were made to feel the slur against our faith and race, which hurt us to our very hearts' core."

The friction between the two groups became more intense as the Irish began to assert themselves in the post–Civil War era. They were particularly good at political organizing, and as their numbers grew, they wrestled for political power with the old-line Boston gentry. Finally, in 1884, the Irish triumphed. Boston, the one-time hub of Puritanism, elected an Irish Catholic mayor. By 1890, the Irish controlled the government of 68 cities and towns in Massachusetts.

At about the same time, the Catholic Church began a drive to remove Catholic children from the public school system and place them in parochial schools. This greatly upset the Protestants, for they felt that the Irish would never be assimilated or trained as "good Americans" if they went to parochial schools. The Yankees wanted to instill proper Anglo-

Saxon virtues and beliefs into the Irish, and were angered to find that the Irish preferred their own culture.

The Irish, on the other hand, felt that their children were being harmed and humiliated in the public schools because of their religion. Parochial schools seemed to be the only solution, although for many years few Irishmen could afford to educate their children this way. The newly created parochial system was expensive, and by 1907 only two-fifths of the children in the Boston Archdiocese were attending parochial schools.

Nevertheless, such clashes between the Irish and the native Americans led many prominent old-line Yankees to believe that the "melting pot" theory was not working too well. It seemed to them that the whole Anglo-Saxon Protestant tradition was in danger of being swept away. More and more Irish were coming into the country every day, and their birth rate was higher than that of the Anglo-Saxons. Furthermore, new immigrants were beginning to come in from southern and eastern Europe—Italians, Poles, Slavs, Jews and such. These groups were regarded as even more inferior than the Irish.

Among the newcomers were radicals, socialists, anarchists and other "undesirables." Immigrant workers were joining the new labor unions, such as the Knights of Labor (formed in 1869) and the American Federation of Labor (founded in 1881). They were involved in a number of bitter and bloody strikes calling for such things as an eight-hour working day, a six-day week, an end to child labor, job security and better wages.

In Chicago, a number of foreign-born anarchists were preaching the forceful overthrow of the government during a nationwide strike in 1886. At one rally in Haymarket Square, the police came in to break up the crowd. But someone threw a bomb, killing seven policemen and wounding 60 spectators.

The public was so enraged that seven anarchists were sentenced to death for preaching violence, even though no one could show that they had anything to do with the bomb throwing.

The Haymarket riot touched off waves of antiforeign hysteria, and caused people to link the labor movement with aliens and anarchists.

Other strikes and riots followed. Several people were killed in 1892 during a strike against the Carnegie Steel Company. In 1894, Eugene Debs led a railroad workers' strike against the Pullman Car Company of Chicago. Mobs on both sides rioted, causing about $80 million worth of damage in the Chicago area. President Grover Cleveland broke the strike by sending 2,000 federal troops into Illinois, and Debs wound up in jail.

People tended to blame the new immigrant workers and radicals for sparking much of the labor unrest. Foreigners were destroying America, they felt.

Out of such fears, the Immigration Restriction League of Boston was born in 1894. Its members came from some of the most prominent New England families, and the chief spokesman for its position in the United States Senate was Henry Cabot Lodge, the same Senator who, years later, would lead the fight against America's entry into the League of Nations.

The Immigration Restriction League's basic goal was to preserve the Anglo-Saxon character of American society on the assumption that Anglo-Saxons were superior to all other groups. Other northern Europeans of Teutonic origins, such as the Germans, Scandinavians and Dutch, were also acceptable. But the "new" immigrants—Italians, Slavs and Jews—were not. The Irish fell somewhere in between.

Branches of the league sprang up in many states, and soon

they were pressing for a bill that would limit immigration for
the first time in American history. Under this bill, no one
would be admitted into the United States unless he could
read and write in his own language. This literacy test would
have kept out large numbers of the "new" immigrants.

The bill passed both Houses of Congress, but it was vetoed
in 1897 by President Grover Cleveland, who angrily refused
to shut America's doors to anyone. The country's old policy
still stood, but its years were numbered.

At this time, America was experiencing the heaviest wave
of immigration in its history. Moreover, the arrival of the
"new" immigrants began to outstrip the arrival of the older
types each year. By 1907, 81 per cent of the immigrants were
coming from southern and eastern Europe. Just 25 years
earlier, the vast majority had been coming from northern and
western Europe.

On the West Coast, immigration of Chinese and, particu-
ularly, Japanese laborers had aroused such hostility that the
United States worked out an informal "Gentlemen's Agreement" with Japan to halt the influx of Japanese.

The "new" immigrants had a more difficult time adjusting
to life in America than their predecessors. The Latins from
Italy, the Slavs and the Jews had less in common with native
Americans than northern Europeans. Their whole style of
life was different. Their clothes, customs and manners
seemed stranger; most of them couldn't speak English
whereas many of the earlier immigrants could; they were
miserably poor; and they crowded into the dirty, sunless
urban ghettos.

They, too, had come to escape the poverty and oppression
of Europe, for they had been even more downtrodden than
previous immigrants (except the Irish). The Jews were fleeing
religious persecution as well as poverty, for thousands were

slaughtered periodically during pogroms in Russia and Poland. They were forced to live in restricted areas, and many occupations were forbidden to them. Hunger was part of their daily lives; in Galicia, 5,000 Jews starved to death each year.

The Jews first started coming to America in the 1870s, but their peak years of immigration were 1900-14. All in all, more than two million Jews—a third of all the Jews in Eastern Europe—eventually sought a haven in the United States. Most of them settled in New York's lower East Side, which became a congested maze of pushcarts, wagons, clothing stalls and peddlers.

Unlike most immigrants, the Jews did not have an agricultural background. In Europe they had been craftsmen, merchants, tailors, shoemakers, jewelers, furriers, etc. In New York large numbers of them found jobs in the garment industry. They spent their days hunched over sewing machines in dark, almost airless sweatshops, or doing piecework in their own crowded homes.

Their religious customs, clothing, diet and language distinctly set them apart from other Americans, but their children became familiar with American ways through the public school system. Many of the children later abandoned the religious orthodoxy of their parents, creating a painful conflict between the generations.

Such clashes between Americanized children and their immigrant parents were common among most of the "new" immigrant groups, as the younger generation struggled to find their place in American society.

Jane Addams, who founded one of the earliest settlement houses in the slums of Chicago, pointed this out in her famous book, *Twenty Years at Hull-House*. In it she says:

From our very first months at Hull-House we found it much easier to deal with the first generation of crowded city life than with the second or third, because it is more natural and cast in a simpler mold. The Italian and Bohemian peasants who live in Chicago, still put on their bright holiday clothes on a Sunday and go to visit their cousins. They tramp along with at least a suggestion of having once walked over plowed fields and breathed country air. The second generation of city poor too often have no holiday clothes and consider their relations a "bad lot." I have heard a drunken man in a maudlin stage, babble of his good country mother and imagine he was driving the cows home, and I knew that his little son who laughed loud at him would be drunk earlier in life and would have no such pastoral interlude to his ravings.

The immigrant parents often had to rely on their children in coping with life in their adopted land. The children spoke English and knew their way about far better than the parents. It was also easier for the Americanized children to get jobs, so that all too often a bright 12- or 13-year-old girl would be earning more than her illiterate father.

This reversal of roles upset the family structure. Children lost respect for their parents, and often they were ashamed of the way they spoke or dressed. Jane Addams recalled one Italian girl who attended cooking classes at Hull-House on the same evenings her mother attended activities there. "Angelina always left her mother at the front door while she herself went around to a side door because she did not wish to be too closely identified in the eyes of the rest of the cooking class with an Italian woman who wore a kerchief over her head, uncouth boots and short petticoats."

Crime and delinquency rates soared among the yearning, discontented children of the immigrants, causing much grief and bewilderment to their parents. The older people remembered their life in Europe and were grateful that in America at least they did not starve. But their children wanted more than that. They wanted nice clothes and better places to live.

Above all, they wanted some fun out of life and tended to rebel against their parents' strict ways.

Native Americans looked upon these "new" immigrants and their problems with growing distaste. They blamed them for the appalling congestion, filth, decay and high crime rate in the urban slums, and they feared them as strange, "degenerate" city dwellers. Earlier immigrants had spread out across the land, settling into a rural way of life that was regarded as more simple and virtuous.

Even more important, many Americans felt that the immigrants' poverty must be their own fault—that if they couldn't get ahead in this great land of opportunity, it must be because they were lazy or stupid or drank too much. In addition, it seemed impossible that these new immigrants could ever be absorbed into American society; they seemed so different from the native stock.

In a sense, these hostile feelings sprang from a clash of different civilizations, with the older, rural Anglo-Saxon population of America on its guard against the strange new foreigners who were pouring into the cities and gaining political control in many urban areas.

The antiforeign feeling turned into near-hysteria during World War I and after the Russian Revolution. Many immigrants still maintained ties with their native lands, including America's wartime enemies and Bolshevik Russia. This aroused doubts about their loyalty and bolstered the movement to stop foreigners from migrating to this country.

In addition, organized labor had begun complaining that the influx of unskilled, foreign workers was hurting the American workingman. There was truth in this, because new arrivals were willing to take any job they could get at very low wages, which tended to keep the general wage level down. With all these antiforeign feelings merging together, America was ready to abandon its traditional policy. In 1921, Congress passed the first bill under which immigrants would be admitted to the United States only under a quota system.

Another bill in 1924 practically halted immigration from southern and eastern Europe, and gave preference to those from the north—the English, Irish, Scandinavians, Germans and Dutch. Twelve out of every 15 immigrants had to come from these countries, primarily to preserve the racial and ethnic composition of the American people.

This discriminatory quota system, with its implication of "superior" and "inferior" races, closed America's gates to thousands of would-be immigrants.

Nevertheless, the last wave of immigration had brought great changes in America. It had made the country far more heterogeneous than ever before, introducing many new nationalities, religions and cultures into American society. It also brought political changes, as more and more urban centers came under the control of new ethnic groups.

(The 1924 immigration policy stood until 1965, when a new law was passed setting an annual quota of 170,000 immigrants from all nations outside the Western Hemisphere, with a limit of 20,000 from any single country. Under this law, no European countries are favored, nor are any discriminated against.)

7

YEARS OF TRANSITION

Sometime between 1900 and 1920 America became an urban nation. The 1920 census showed for the first time that more Americans were living in cities than in rural areas. This was partly because of the large masses of immigrants pouring into the cities, and partly because of the younger people who were leaving their farms and villages to head for the urban centers.

This population shift was just one of many changes that were revolutionizing the comfortable old "American way of life." The America of 1920 was vastly different from the America of 1900, for in these 20 years the country became urbanized and industrialized at a dizzying pace.

When the 20th century dawned, America's heart still lay in its small towns and villages. There people still lived a relatively simple existence, isolated from the social chaos, troubles and turmoils of the large cities. But they were also cut off from the stimulation of urban intellectual and cultural life, so that their ideas and attitudes tended to remain fixed. Most people in small towns knew one another all their lives. They went to the same schools, worked together and went to church together on Sundays. There were few outside influences on their lives. Although their world was comfortable and secure, it was also often sterile, uninspiring and conformist.

For the most part, there wasn't too much contact between city people and country people. For a family in a small rural village, a trip to the city was a big event requiring elaborate preparations. It was not something that people did every day or even every year. Nor did city people know much about country life. Children growing up in the slums of Chicago or New York might never even see a live chicken or a cow.

By 1920, however, a variety of new inventions had brought rural and urban America much closer together. Perhaps the most important of these inventions was the "Tin Lizzie"— the affectionate nickname for Henry Ford's first low-priced, mass-produced Model T.

More than any other man, Henry Ford put America on wheels. This cranky, self-willed mechanical genius went against every common business practice of his time to make sure that the average workingman could afford one of his cars. Other businessmen thought he was crazy, but it wasn't long before they were imitating his methods.

Ford had always been a maverick, even as a boy. His parents owned a small farm near Dearborn, Michigan, and Henry and his brothers were doing farm chores from the time they were very young. Their parents assumed that when they grew up they would get land of their own and become farmers, too.

But Henry hated farming. He also didn't care much for school, and barely learned how to read and write. All his life he remained only semiliterate. The only thing young Henry really liked was working with tools and machines. In this respect he was a genius, for he could figure out how something worked almost as soon as he saw it in use.

Henry rebelled against farming and left home at the age of

16. For a while he worked as a mechanic and clock repairman in Detroit, Michigan, but later on he got a much better job as an engineer for the Edison Illuminating Company. He advanced rapidly and soon became chief engineer. Although it seemed as if his future lay with the company, his heart really wasn't in it. He had another all-consuming interest.

In the yard behind his rented house in Detroit, he had built a little machine shop, where he spent all his evenings. He was trying to build a horseless carriage that would be propelled by a gasoline-powered motor.

The idea was not new. Others in Europe and America were also experimenting with such machines. In Europe they were called motorcars or automobiles. In America, the first such car was built in Springfield, Massachusetts, in 1892 by the Duryea brothers.

Ford, working in his little brick shed with makeshift tools and materials, had one failure after another. Nevertheless, he kept on working night after night, and became known around the neighborhood as "Crazy Henry."

One night in the spring of 1896, Henry Ford finished his first car. But when he tried to drive it out of the shed, he found it was too big—it wouldn't fit through the door.

In a wild rage, he picked up an ax and knocked out part of the wall. By 4 A.M., he finally got the car out of the shed and drove it around the block. It was a great success.

After that, Henry Ford could often be seen driving his "mechanical toy" through the streets of Detroit, followed by a string of curious boys and barking dogs.

During the next few years he built two more cars which were improvements on his original model. By this time, several firms were producing automobiles, but the price was so high that only the very rich could afford them. Cars became a popular plaything for the wealthy, but average people weren't very interested in them. They regarded them as a silly, useless extravagance, another trinket for the rich to waste their money on. It seemed almost sinful for anyone to buy such a costly, frivolous gadget. The automobile offended the Puritan notion of thrift. Henry Ford felt this way, too. He disliked pomp and extravagance and scorned the rich, for he had been brought up in the Calvinist tradition. While other firms were catering to the wealthy, he wanted to build a car that would be cheap enough for the ordinary man.

By 1903, he had interested a number of people in his ideas and raised a small amount of capital—about $28,000. With this, he started the Ford Motor Company in Detroit.

The firm's first car was a gaily colored little "runabout" called the Model A, or Fordmobile, that sold for $800. However, this was not the cheapest car on the market. The Merry Oldsmobile was selling for $650. The price of most cars, though, was about $2,000. The 1904 Cadillac sold for $7,000.

The Model A was moderately successful, but Ford was not wholly satisfied with it. He was still experimenting with other techniques and designs, including the Model B touring car at $2,000, and the Model C four-seater at $950. Over the next few years, he worked all the way through Model S, which was the last of the experimental cars.

By 1908, Ford knew exactly what he wanted. He embodied all his ideas and knowledge in the Model T, and announced that from then on, the Ford Motor Company would produce just this one model. What's more, he said, "any customer can have a car painted any color that he wants so long as it is black."

This was unheard of in marketing circles! Every manufacturer gave his customers some choice of style or color, no matter what the product. But Ford was going to put out just one type of car in black only. Furthermore, he said, the design would remain the same year after year so that he could produce cars more efficiently and keep lowering the price.

This was something else that manufacturers didn't do, but Ford felt that by cutting the price he would sell more cars— and earn his profits through high volume rather than high prices.

His intent, he said, was to "build a motorcar for the great multitude. It will be large enough for the family, but small enough for the individual to run and care for. It will be constructed of the best materials, by the best men to be hired, after the simplest designs that modern engineering can devise. But it will be so low in price that no man making a good salary will be unable to own one—and enjoy with his family the blessing of hours of pleasure in God's great open spaces."

To produce the Model T in great quantity, Ford needed more space. He bought 60 acres of land in Highland Park outside Detroit and built a new factory. There he concentrated on improving mass production techniques so that he could bring prices down.

Over the next five years, Henry Ford developed the assembly line and conveyor belt system that was soon to become the standard method for mass production all over America. Under this system, goods could be produced so cheaply that thousands of once-costly items were brought within reach of the average family, helping to give Americans the highest standard of living in the world.

Ford did not invent this system all by himself. It was based partly on Eli Whitney's original division-of-labor method and his discovery of how to make interchangeable parts. The assembly line idea had been used by a number of manufacturers, beginning with Cyrus McCormick in his Chicago reaper plant. Conveyor belts had also been used before, although on a limited basis.

What Ford did was to put all these things together, and

refine and systemize them until he had the most efficient manufacturing plant in the country. The basic ideas behind it were simple: first, that the work must always be brought to the man by means of a conveyor so that he did not have to waste time running about to get anything; second, that no worker should ever have to stoop or bend down to attach anything for this, too, would slow the production.

The operation was divided into subassemblies for the various parts of the car, such as the radiator or the steering wheel, and the main assembly line, where the parts were put together in 45 steps and a whole car emerged.

As Ford described it, "Some men do only one or two operations, others do more. The man who places a part does not fasten it—the part may not be fully in place until after several operations later. The man who puts in a bolt does not put on the nut; the man who puts on the nut does not tighten it. On operation number 34 the budding motor gets its gasoline . . . on operation number 44 the radiator is filled with water, and on operation number 45 the car drives out. . . ."

This is basically how a modern, mass-production assembly plant works. The system has been praised for the great abundance of cheap goods it can produce; at the same time, it has been damned for its effect on factory workers. The monotony of standing in one place and repeating the same simple function over and over again left workers numb and drained at the end of the day. There was no feeling of satisfaction or achievement from their work, because each man's task was so far removed from the end product. Under the old handicraft system, workers at least got a sense of accomplishment from having made a complete item by themselves. They could take pride in their work and feel themselves the equal of any man. But the more a job was mechanized and divided, the less pride each worker could take in it. Ford had carried the division of labor to such an extreme that workers were reduced to robotlike creatures.

On the other hand, a man didn't need any skills to work on an assembly line. As this type of factory system expanded, it opened up many more jobs for unskilled workers. The masses of unskilled immigrants who were pouring into America during the early years of the 20th century often got their start as factory workers. They didn't have to know how to read or write to work in a factory, nor did they need any mechanical skills or previous factory experience. In fact, Ford preferred inexperienced machine-tool operators who would have nothing to unlearn, who would just do as they were told, over and over again, from bell-time to bell-time.

However, the turnover in the new Ford plant was very high because of the monotony of the work. Partly to combat this, Ford made an announcement on January 5, 1914, that shook the entire country. He said he would raise wages in his plant to a minimum of $5 a day for an eight-hour working day!

This was more than double what the average unskilled factory worker was earning at that time, and there was a near riot at Highland Park the next day when 10,000 workers descended upon the Ford plant seeking jobs. Finally, police had to break up the mob by turning water hoses on them.

Businessmen were furious with Ford. They accused him of ruining the labor market and putting crazy ideas into workers' heads. But Ford knew what he was doing. In addition to stimulating his workers, he also had the notion that if more Americans earned higher wages, they would be able to buy more industrial products, including cars. As part of this same notion, he kept lowering the price of his Model T. When it was first produced in 1909, it sold for $950. Year after year, Ford cut the price, until by 1924 it had dropped to $290.

Ford made a fortune from his Model T. At the same time, he introduced a new, democratic approach to business. Instead of paying workers starvation wages and producing luxury goods for the wealthy, he showed that it was good business sense to pay workers well enough so that they could buy the factory goods they were producing. In this way there would be a large demand for goods, and everyone would benefit. Capitalists could profit from a high volume of sales, rather than from high prices and low wages, and workers could enjoy the fruits of their labor.

Today, most American businesses follow this principle to some degree, although they may have been pushed and prodded into it by labor unions. Working-class Americans own television sets, washing machines, automobiles and countless other luxuries that workers in other countries still cannot afford. But in America, advanced capitalism depends on a heavy demand among all classes of people for mass-produced goods. In short, if workers aren't buying cars, business slumps in Detroit.

The automobile changed the face of America. With the sturdy, practical Model T leading the way, cars became a familiar sight all across the country. Most roads weren't suited for automobiles, however, so new and better roads were needed to accommodate the growing number of cars. Today's vast network of superhighways and paved roads was built to serve the automobile.

New towns sprang up along the new roads, and one city in particular owed its spectacular growth to the automobile— Detroit. When Henry Ford first built his backyard workshop there, Detroit was just another busy little town. But it soon became the automobile-manufacturing capital of the world, providing jobs for hundreds of thousands of workers and shipping out millions of cars. All sorts of related industries were also drawn to Detroit, so that in a very short time it became the nation's fifth largest city.

Today, about 10 million Americans are directly or indirectly employed in the manufacture, sale or maintenance of automobiles. The automobile is crucial to our whole economy, for so many other industries depend heavily on it, like the steel, copper and rubber industries.

Motels, roadside diners, shopping centers, gas stations—all were products of the automobile age. For the farmer, the automobile was particularly important. It revolutionized his whole way of life by bringing him out of isolation. A trip to the nearest town or city became commonplace once he had an automobile. As one farm wife said when asked why her family owned a car but not a bathtub: "Why, you can't go to town in a bathtub!"

It wasn't long before people in rural areas began to think of the car as a necessity rather than a luxury. It brought them closer to towns, and it brought towns closer to each other. People became familiar with the entire region surrounding them instead of just their own immediate little village. They no longer had to rely on the nearby country general store for all their needs. The whole family could hop into their car and drive 10 or 15 miles for clothes, shoes or entertainment. A man might even live in one town and work in another.

On the whole, the automobile helped break down the sense of separateness in rural towns and villages. Towns in the same general region became more like each other as people traveled freely among them.

Rural people also became more familiar with city life as their cars gave them a cheap, convenient means of reaching the big urban centers. By expanding people's horizons this way, the car also helped accelerate the flight of the population from the farms to the cities.

Farming techniques were also affected by the invention of the car. The technical know-how that went into the making of cars was soon applied to the tractor. "Old Dobbin" was put out to pasture as enterprising farmers hitched up their plows to motorized tractors and speeded across their fields. The mechanization of agriculture, which had begun in the previous century, took a huge leap forward as farm machinery became motorized. Farms grew larger and larger, and less manpower was needed to work the land.

Another invention based on the automobile also came into use at this time—the motor truck. Whereas before railroads had had a virtual monopoly on large-scale shipments of goods over land, now the motor truck loomed as a deadly rival.

Both rural and urban America were on wheels now, giving Americans far greater mobility than ever before. Just as railroads had helped pull this vast country together by linking region to region, the car had a similar unifying effect.

So did other inventions of this era. In 1903, Americans saw the first moving picture that told a complete story, *The Great Train Robbery*. About two years later, the first nickelodeons appeared. These forerunners of movie theaters were often clumsily set up in vacant stores or other available places. By 1910, about 10,000 motion picture theaters had sprung up across the nation. As the early silent movies became more popular, they helped shape the tastes and habits of the American people.

A Kansas farmer and his wife could get in their car on a Saturday night and drive to the nearest large town to see a movie—perhaps the same movie that a New York garment worker, a Pennsylvania coal miner or a Chicago businessman was also seeing that evening. There they could all sympathize with the poor but beautiful heroine, hiss the mustachioed villain, cheer the dashing leading man and walk out secure in the knowledge that good always triumphs over evil. The next morning, the farmer's wife, the businessman's wife and the miner's wife might all take a little extra time with their hair, trying to imitate the style worn by the lovely heroine. They might have also noticed her dress, and might look for one similar to it the next time they shopped for clothes. Even though they lived in different parts of the country and had different levels of income, they had shared the same experience and were influenced by it.

In this way, the movies helped influence nationwide trends, whether in clothing, furniture, hair styles, manners or morals. If a leading lady wore lipstick but still lived happily ever after at the end of the movie, then perhaps lipstick was not so sinful after all.

Movies also introduced people to life-styles that were different from their own. People in the East could see what a Western ranch looked like; the poor could see how millionaires lived and behaved; small-town people could see what city life was like. They could see re-enactments of historical events, such as D. W. Griffith's big Civil War spectacular of 1915, *The Birth of a Nation*. Of course, moviegoers were also exposed to the distortions and prejudices of the moviemakers —the Ku Klux Klan emerged as the heroes of *The Birth of a Nation*—so movies could also be blamed for helping to spread false images and stereotypes.

New fashions, styles and ideas were being spread by another means, too—magazines. Prior to the 1890s, there were no low-priced magazines geared to a mass audience. Magazines were usually directed towards small groups of readers with specific interests.

But the turn of the century saw the rise of the mass-circulation magazines. Publishers had discovered that by selling magazines for a very low price, they could get a very large audience—and this would attract advertisers. Then profits would come from advertising revenues, rather than from sales of the magazine.

Among the earliest of the mass-circulation magazines were *McClure's, Munsey's,* the *Saturday Evening Post* and the *Ladies' Home Journal.* The *Post* cost 5¢ and the *Journal* 10¢, and both were selling well over one million copies per issue during the first decades of the 20th century. By 1922, the *Post's* circulation had reached 2,187,024, with advertising revenues of $28,278,755.

All of these magazines helped spread middle-class ideas and styles of living among millions of Americans, whether they lived in the city or the country, East or West, North or South. The *Journal* prided itself on inspiring "good taste" in such matters as dress, home furnishings and architecture, while the other magazines were geared to the everyday interests of average middle-class citizens.

Their advertisements introduced Americans to the promised joys of many products, such as cars, typewriters, breakfast foods and corsets, all of which were first being produced on a mass basis. In this way, the magazines helped awaken desires among all classes of people for manufactured products.

Through cars, movies and magazines, people everywhere began to have far more in common with each other than before. They were being exposed to similar ideas and information. A Maine fisherman and a California rancher might both read the *Saturday Evening Post,* and they might both decide to try Toasted Corn Flakes by Kellogg as a result of seeing the ads. Almost everyone in the country could recognize Charlie Chaplin or Lillian Gish.

The telephone, too, was bringing people closer together. Friends or relatives who lived too far away to see each other regularly could now have a conversation without even leaving their homes. They could exchange opinions and gossip from day to day, thereby keeping up with events in each other's town or city.

This was also the era of great industrial and technological advances. Between 1900 and 1920, the nation's output of steel and iron tripled. Electric power was being used more widely, particularly for business and industry. The first skyscrapers went up in New York, beginning in 1908 with the 41-story Singer building, then the 50-story Metropolitan Tower and, in 1913, the 60-story Woolworth building. Without steel for structural strength or electricity for their vital elevator service, these architectural wonders could never have been built.

Chain stores also became part of the everyday scene around this time. A&P food stores and the Woolworth 5¢ and 10¢ stores both seized on the idea of low prices and very high sales volume as a way of making profits. By operating hundreds of stories in one chain, they could place huge orders at special rates, keep their prices lower than anyone else and attract millions of shoppers. Both chains were enormously successful. By 1924, A&P was operating 11,413 food stores around the country.

In 1903, Wilbur and Orville Wright opened up vast new horizons for mankind with their first brief airplane flight, but the idea of man's being able to fly still seemed so absurd that people didn't pay much attention. It wasn't until 1908 that newspapers took the idea seriously enough to give full coverage to the Wright brothers' activities. Even then, it was decades before airplanes became a common means of travel.

Wireless telegraphy was also in its infancy at the turn of the century. But by the 1920s it had given birth to the idea of radio—the first form of live entertainment that could be brought right into people's living rooms.

All in all, the first 20 years of the new century marked the beginning of modern America as we know it today. From its agrarian origins, America had sprouted into an industrialized, urban nation, producing goods on a mass basis for great multitudes of people.

But the changes had come about so quickly that most Americans couldn't really grasp what had happened. Even though the majority now lived in cities, America still thought of itself as rural—a nation of small, closely knit, picture-postcard towns. Despite all the physical and social changes, rural attitudes and habits still dominated the political scene. The Puritan virtues of thrift, hard work and self-reliance meant that most Americans were still against such things as high government spending or government controls over business activities and working conditions.

In the early part of the century, when the abuses of big business first became clear, there was a brief attempt at reform. President Theodore Roosevelt started his crusade against the "malefactors of great wealth" and their monopolies, while muckrakers like Ida Tarbell, Lincoln Steffens and Upton Sinclair exposed the raw underbelly of business and government.

But the outbreak of World War I halted the reform movement. Industry was pressed to turn out enormous quantities of goods for the war effort, and attention was riveted overseas.

Afterwards, the fears aroused by the Russian Revolution abroad and by aliens, anarchists and socialists at home brought on a wave of political repression. People were jailed for advocating politically unpopular causes; immigration from southern and eastern Europe was practically halted; and the country turned inward and refused to join the League of Nations.

Americans were tired of the chaos, confusion and upheavals of the 20th century. They wanted to go back to the good old days, and they voted for Warren G. Harding for President because he promised a "return to normalcy."

By "normalcy," he and most Americans seemed to mean the old small-town way of life, with its comfortable security and stability. Under Harding, the federal government didn't even try to cope with the problems of a modern urban-industrial society. The free-enterprise system was left to work out its kinks without government interference, and most people thought this was the way it should be. "That government is best which governs least" was still the nation's motto, even though America had changed from a place of self-sufficient towns and villages to an industrial giant whose economic health was shaky.

After the war, America had gone through a staggering inflation followed by a recession. Farmers were in trouble. Their new machinery and techniques were producing a surplus of crops, so prices had dropped sharply. But Harding and his successor, Calvin Coolidge, did nothing to offset these problems.

Coolidge, in particular, was fond of saying, "If you see ten troubles coming down the road, you can be sure that nine will run into the ditch before they reach you, and you have to battle with only one of them."

Among the troubles he thought would "run into the ditch" was the hyperactivity of the stock market. Too many people were buying too many shares of speculative stocks on borrowed money. The stock market was running high and wild, but it was a paper prosperity only. Coolidge noted the danger, but he felt that the regulation of the New York Stock Exchange was New York's business, not the federal government's.

Similarly, he relaxed existing regulations on business because he felt that if business was thriving, America as a whole would prosper. "The business of America is business," he said. So he lowered business taxes and kept high tariffs to protect American industries.

Meanwhile, the railroads were having severe difficulties, brought on by the competition of trucks and automobiles. During Harding's administration there were also many labor problems, particularly in the coal and railroad industries. Harding tried to deal with them, but was unsuccessful. When Coolidge was faced with similar labor crises, he dumped them in the lap of subordinates.

While these and other grave problems simmered above and below the surface, America danced and drank its way through the frivolous '20s (despite Prohibition). Women lifted their skirts, cut their hair and announced their emancipation. They drank and smoked in public, and they found a new idol in that wicked movie vamp, Theda Bara. A revolution in manners and morals was taking place that seemed to overshadow the deeper social and economic changes of the 20th century.

President Herbert Hoover, more foresighted and progressive than his predecessors, was alert to the economic danger signals. But by then it was too late.

Disaster struck in 1929. With the onset of the Great Depression, thousands of banks, businesses and farms went under. It was only then that people realized how interdependent the economy had become—that if one or two major industries collapsed, the rest would also topple.

Goods that people could not afford piled up in the stores and warehouses. Production slowed down, factories closed and more and more people were thrown out of work.

The old American dream—that success could come to anyone who was willing to work hard and was thrifty and self-reliant—simply did not work in an urban-industrial setting. In complex, modern America, people found that their well-being depended more on their society and less on their own efforts. If there were no jobs to be had, they could not work; if people couldn't afford to buy goods, others had to stop producing them. This was far different from the days when a man could clear a piece of land for himself and make out all right strictly through his own efforts. In the modern world, man more often had to rely on others for his livelihood and take whatever wages he could get.

The effects of the Depression were felt more strongly in the large urban centers and industrial areas than in the small towns and villages. Farmers suffered greatly, but the rest of the rural population was not as badly off as city workers.

In the election of 1932, America finally caught up with all the industrial and social changes that had been taking place over the years. The old small-town attitudes that had dominated political thinking were swept aside as the urban majority joined with the Solid South to support Franklin Delano Roosevelt's sweeping social welfare programs.

The people were ready for a government that would step in and act, even though this meant a radical change from all previous governments. They had come to realize that the old "hands off, do-nothing," policy was just not suitable for a highly industrialized economy. New political and social beliefs were springing up out of the urban-industrial experience rather than rural life. For the first time, urban America would have an urban-minded government.

During Roosevelt's many years as President, he completely altered the role of the federal government in American life. The government was into everything now; no sphere of the economy was left untouched. In an effort to spark economic recovery, the government spent more than it ever had before; it created jobs for large numbers of people; it provided for social security and other welfare measures; it subsidized farmers; it outlawed child labor; it set maximum hours and minimum wages for many workers. The list went on and on.

Many people were outraged by Roosevelt's actions. They

accused him of destroying the American way of life and socializing the country. But a far greater number of Americans chose to stay with him, re-electing him three more times. He was President longer than any other man. During his 12 years in office he set the federal government on a new course that, even if it didn't always succeed, was at least geared to the needs of a modern industrial, urbanized nation.

By the time of World War II, rural and urban America had grown much alike on the surface. People dressed in the same styles, saw the same movies, rode around in cars, shopped in the same type of supermarkets, followed the same fads and used the same products. America had developed a mass culture shared by city and country people alike. But fundamental differences still remained.

The large cities were made up of many working-class ethnic and racial minorities who voted Democratic, supported labor unions, pressed for more social welfare measures, etc. Their way of thinking stemmed from industrial conditions. Since they formed a majority, they controlled national policies as well as their own city governments.

The rural population, on the other hand, still consisted largely of white, Anglo-Saxon Protestants. They voted Republican, disliked government interference with their lives and were more conservative and more resistant to change than their city counterparts. Their way of thinking stemmed from rural, small-town conditions. Although they were now in the minority, they still controlled most state governments because voting districts were seldom redrawn to reflect population changes. This meant that most state governments were much more conservative than the federal government.

Essentially, the same division still exists in American society today. Because of it, the cities are constantly being short-changed by the state governments, which are still dominated by rural voters. On the whole, city people get less state aid per capita than rural people for such matters as education, health services, welfare measures and public works. This situation has had much to do with the serious financial troubles that most cities are plagued with today.

part two

Crisis in the Cities

8

NORTH TO THE
PROMISED LAND

In the introduction to his book *Manchild in the Promised Land*, Claude Brown says,

I want to talk about the first Northern urban generation of Negroes. I want to talk about the experiences of a misplaced generation, of a misplaced people in an extremely complex, confused society. . . .

The characters are sons and daughters of former Southern sharecroppers. These were the poorest people of the South, who poured into New York City during the decade following the Great Depression. These migrants were told that unlimited opportunities for prosperity existed in New York and that there was no "color problem" there. They were told that Negroes lived in houses with bathrooms, electricity, running water and indoor toilets. To them, this was the 'promised land' that Mammy had been singing about in the cotton fields for many years. . . .

It seems that Cousin Willie, in his lying haste, had neglected to tell the folks down home about one of the most important aspects of the promised land: it was a slum ghetto. There was a tremendous difference in the way life was lived up North. There were too many people full of hate and bitterness crowded into a dirty, stinky, uncared-for closet-size section of a great city. . . .

The children of these disillusioned colored pioneers inherited the total lot of their parents—the disappointments, the anger. To add to their misery, they had little hope of deliverance. For where does one run to when he's already in the promised land?

The first wave of black migration to the Northern urban centers took place during World War I. Until that time there were only small pockets of Negro settlements in the North. The overwhelming majority of Negroes lived in the rural areas of the South, working mainly as sharecroppers on land owned by whites.

Under the most common form of sharecropping, the worker was hired to live on and farm a piece of land assigned to him by the owner. In return for his labor, the worker received a share of what he grew, usually about half the crop. In addition, on many farms, the tenant also had to be available to work on the landlord's "home farm" for a small cash wage. During the slack season in the autumn and early winter, the owner provided his tenants with food so that they would be on hand when it was time to start a new crop. The system was used mainly for crops that required a great deal of hand labor, such as tobacco, cotton and peanuts.

As sharecroppers, the Negroes and poor white farm tenants were no better off than feudal serfs. But in addition to the economic exploitation, Southern Negroes were severely oppressed in many other ways. They were prevented from voting. They had almost no rights in Southern courts of law. The testimony of black witnesses carried no weight whatsoever, except if they were testifying against other blacks. If a white man assaulted or even killed a Negro, he usually got off without being punished. But if a Negro killed a white man, even in self-defense, he was certain to be executed.

Lynchings were widespread, so that the fear of lynching kept Negroes in a constant state of terror and submission.

The Savannah, Georgia, *Morning News* commented in 1917: "There is scarcely a Negro mother in the country who does not live in dread and fear that her husband or son may come in unfriendly contact with some white person so as to bring the lynchers or the arresting officers to her door, which may result in the wiping out of her entire family. It must be acknowledged that this is a sad condition."

In addition, Negroes were often sent to jail for petty offenses or no offense at all. Southern sheriffs in many places received a fee for feeding their prisoners; the more prisoners they had, the greater their income. For example, in Jefferson County, Alabama, the sheriff made a net profit of about $25,000 a year for four years. He was receiving 30¢ a day for feeding each prisoner, but actually he fed them for 10¢ a day. Wherever this type of fee system existed, Negroes were often rounded up and arrested for no reason other than to enrich the local sheriff.

Schools for black children were notoriously bad. The teachers were untrained, and the school buildings were in wretched condition, without proper sanitation, lighting or necessary equipment. In one county in Mississippi, where 60 per cent of the school children were Negro, only two schools were provided for them—but there were seven schools for the white children. A teacher in a white school taught about 30 pupils a term; a teacher in a black school taught about 100.

Despite the extreme oppression, Negroes had remained in the South because they couldn't get a foothold in the North. Industry was closed to them. Northern manufacturers and industrialists were getting a large supply of cheap, unskilled labor from the masses of immigrants who were pouring into the country each year. As the older immigrants worked their way up into the better jobs, the menial positions were easily refilled by the newer immigrants.

Negroes who had gone up North worked mainly as domestic servants or as shoe shine boys, waiters, porters, dishwashers and the like. There was no real opportunity for them in other fields as long as white immigrant labor was available.

But within three years after the outbreak of World War I in Europe, more than 400,000 blacks migrated to the North. As the movement continued into the 1920s, the total climbed to about one million.

There were several reasons for this sudden exodus. First of all, the agricultural revolution had reached the deep South, so that poor whites and Negroes were beginning to be pushed off the land. Then, in the summers of 1915 and 1916, the boll weevil struck throughout the Cotton Kingdom, doing great damage to the crops. The market price of cotton fell, creating an economic slump in the South. Heavy floods during the summer of 1915 added to the misery.

With the outbreak of World War I in Europe, the price of food and other basic goods began to rise throughout the country. But farm wages in the South did not rise. The average farm laborer continued to earn only about 75¢ a day, while the prices of things he needed to buy kept on rising.

With much of the cotton crop destroyed, many farmers could not afford to support their sharecroppers between growing seasons. Many of these tenant farmers were dismissed in the fall, and had no way of supporting themselves until spring planting time. Also, a number of farmers turned to other crops after the boll weevil ravaged their cotton fields. This, too, left many sharecroppers out of work because the growing of cotton required about five times as many workers as the cultivation of most other crops.

For Southern Negroes, who lived under deplorable conditions even in good times, the new turn of events was intolerable.

But during this same period, events were taking place in the North that would greatly affect their lives. When the war

broke out, many immigrants were called back home to fight
for their native lands. The war disrupted everything, and immigration slowed to a trickle.

For the first time, Northern manufacturers and industrialists found themselves without a supply of cheap labor. In
addition, many industries were under pressure to turn out
more goods than ever before to fill the government's war
needs. The remaining immigrant workers moved up to fill
higher positions, leaving jobs on the lowest levels vacant.

Firms that had never hired Negroes, and swore they never
would, now needed Negro help. They began advertising in
Negro newspapers and sending agents down South to recruit
workers. The railroads were particularly active this way. Their
agents gave out free railroad passes to enable poor Negroes
to migrate north and go to work for the railroad companies.
Many Negroes used the free passes, but then looked for better
paying jobs elsewhere.

Wages in the North seemed incredible to Southern Negroes, who found themselves earning double or triple what
they had made back home. In the Southern lumber mills,
railroad shops, oil mills and cotton compresses, unskilled Negroes earned only about $1 to $1.50 per day. But in the Northern industries they were taking home between $2.50 and $3.75
per day. Negro women, who earned about $2.50 *a week* as
domestic servants in the South, could earn that much in a
single day up North.

To sharecroppers who had never earned more than 75¢ a
day for back-breaking labor, the North seemed like "the promised land." A farm laborer, reading the leading Negro newspaper, the *Chicago Defender*, would gape at ads like these:

Men wanted at once. Good steady employment for colored.
Thirty and 39½¢ per hour. Weekly payments. Good warm sanitary quarters free. Best commissary privileges. Towns of Newark

and Jersey City. Fifteen minutes by car line offer cheap and suitable homes for men with families. For out of town parties of ten or more cheap transportation will be arranged. Only reliable men who stay on their job are wanted. 3,000 laborers to work on railroad. Factory hires all race help. More positions open than men for them. Laborers wanted for foundry, warehouse and yard work. Excellent opportunity to learn trades, paying good money. Start $2.50—$2.75 per day. Extra for overtime. Transportation advanced for Chicago only. Apply Chicago League on Urban Conditions Among Negroes.

The *Chicago Defender* was one of the main forces behind the northward migration. This newspaper had a wide circulation in the South, and was considered militant for its time. It ceaselessly urged the Southern black man to reject the lowly status forced upon him by the white man. The only way Negroes could achieve their rights, it declared, was by leaving the South.

However, many Negroes were afraid to go North at first for fear of the cold. They had heard stories of Negroes freezing to death on the streets, to which the *Defender* retorted:

To die from the bite of frost is far more glorious than at the hands of a mob. I beg you, my brother, to leave the benighted land. You are a free man. Show the world that you will not let false leaders lead you. Your neck has been in the yoke. Will you continue to keep it there because some "white folks' nigger" wants you to? Leave for all quarters of the globe. Get out of the South. Your being there in the numbers in which you are gives the southern politician too strong a hold on your progress. . . .

These were inflammatory words for that era. The *Defender* expressed all the anger and resentment that Southern black men felt but dared not show for fear of being lynched. At the same time, the *Defender* inspired dreams of a better future for black people, if only they would go north.

And so they went. In some sections, whole villages were nearly emptied as Negroes poured onto the trains for the journey north. It was like an epidemic. People sold their possessions for almost nothing and left with little more than the clothes on their back. Abandoned houses and farms were seen everywhere.

Just like the European immigrants before them, these first migrants sent letters back home telling of the glories in the new world. One woman from Hattiesburg, Mississippi, was said to have sent such a persuasive letter that it lured 200 people away from the town.

Another Hattiesburg man wrote this letter to a friend:

Mike, old boy, I was promoted on the first of the month. I was made first assistant to the head carpenter. When he is out of place I take everything in charge and was raised to $95 per month. You know I know my stuff. What's the news generally around H'burg? I should have been here twenty years ago. I just begin to feel like a man. It's a great deal of pleasure in knowing that you have got some privileges. My children are going to the same school with the whites and I don't have to humble to no one. I have registered. Will vote the next election and there isn't any "yes sir and no, sir." It's all yes and no, and no, Sam, and Bill.

If those who stayed behind thought such stories were exaggerations at first, they changed their minds when they saw that some migrants were able to send money back home, sometimes as much as $30 every two weeks.

In Mississippi, it was estimated that half the Negroes who left did so at the urging of friends and relatives through letters.

The Negro migration came as a shock to Southern whites. Now it was they who found themselves short of help. Within a year or two after the exodus had begun, white farmers in some sections were having a hard time finding workers to harvest their crops. Homes were without servants, and some shops and mills couldn't even function because of the lack of workers.

One Georgia plantation was particularly hard hit. More than 15 Negro families had been living on it as sharecroppers. They were treated badly by the absentee owner, who lived in town and visited the farm once a week. The sharecroppers received only a small allowance for food and clothing each month during the slack season, no matter how many children they had to support. When the money ran out, they were left with nothing until the following month. They were afraid to leave their farms and take odd jobs to tide them over because the landlord would have been furious.

One day, when the owner came to visit his plantation, he was shocked to find all the homes and farms deserted except one, where two old men were living. They told him that all the others had got free railroad passes and headed north, while they alone had remained loyal. As a reward, he gave them some extra money and left thinking that at least they would be there to watch over his plantation. By the next morning they were gone. They hadn't been able to get free passes like the others because they were too old to be hired as workers. But with their "reward" money, they bought their own railroad tickets and joined their friends up North.

Stories like this were repeated throughout the South, and it wasn't long before state and county officials tried to halt the migration. Some Southern states banned the *Chicago Defender*, so it had to be distributed clandestinely. Even so its circulation continued to rise, going from about 50,000 in 1915 to 125,000 in 1918.

Elsewhere, recruiting agents from the North were being run out of town, so they, too, began operating under cover. A common practice was for an agent to stroll casually along the streets of some bustling Southern town where he wouldn't be easily noticed. When passing groups of Negroes he wouldn't even look at them, but would say in a low voice, "Anyone who wants to get to Chicago, see me at——."

Everyone seemed to be leaving, so that those who stayed behind felt the despair and loneliness of being left out. One woman from a small, half-emptied Mississippi town said that the worst part was having to pass all the vacant houses of old friends who were up North and prospering. "There ain't enough people I still know here to give me a decent burial," she said.

But there were some benefits for those who stayed behind. The labor shortage brought about a rise in wages throughout the South. In Savannah, Georgia, wages for unskilled labor rose by about 50 per cent; in Thomasville, Georgia, they went up by 100 per cent. Towns and cities elsewhere in the South experienced similar wage increases, and the pay for farm laborers also shot up.

In addition, some Southern towns and counties were alarmed enough to try to improve living conditions for the Negroes in the hope that this would induce them to stay. Some dilapidated Negro schools were treated to their first coat of paint. Southern officials suddenly noticed the unsanitary conditions that existed in long-neglected Negro sections, and set about to improve them. The number of lynchings and arbitrary arrests declined, and on the whole, Negroes were treated less harshly than before—as long as the migration lasted.

But the North was not all that it had seemed to be. Although jobs were plentiful, and many Negro migrants were making more money than they had ever seen before, Northern city life was not very pleasant for them.

Housing was the worst problem. In Chicago, the hub of the northward movement, Negroes had been concentrated in a small area on the South Side. When 50,000 Negroes suddenly poured into the city in a year and a half (between January, 1916, and July, 1917), there was a frantic scramble for living space. The Chicago Urban League reported that in just one day there were 664 Negro applicants for houses, and only 50 of them succeeded in renting anything.

Chicago's whites put up a fierce struggle when Negroes tried to rent in their neighborhoods. Although European immigrants had also faced discrimination in housing, the black man was more visible than other newcomers. If Negroes moved into a block their presence would be obvious at once, so the resistance against them was fierce. Wherever they did make inroads, the whites usually abandoned the neighborhood in a short time.

The congestion was appalling. So was the rent-gouging. Rates for Negro housing rose by about 30 per cent, and in some cases jumped as high as 50 per cent, so that even with his higher wages the Negro was still poor.

Whole families crowded together, so that there might be as many as 15 people living in just two small, dark rooms. The already run-down Negro neighborhoods turned into horrid, decaying slums under the strain of such overcrowding, and disease spread rapidly.

The situation was the same in other Northern cities where large numbers of Negroes had migrated. In New Jersey, one newspaper said of the newcomers:

Unused to city life, crowded into dark rooms, their clothing and household utensils unsuitable, the stoves they have bought all being too small to heat even the tiny rooms they have procured (the installment houses are charging from $20 to $30 for these stoves), shivering with the cold from which they do not know how to protect themselves, it is small wonder that illness has overtaken large numbers.

Coming from a region where they had enjoyed a mild climate and ample space, if little else, rural blacks found Northern city life oppressive. In addition to the horror of slum living, Northern cities were unfriendly, lonely and bewildering places.

Rural Negroes had been used to a more simple, close-knit way of life that often centered around church activities. To many Negroes, the church was the most important thing in their lives, and it exerted a strong influence over their behavior. Those who violated its standards were in danger of being excluded from church affairs, which was a terrible disgrace. Also, in a small community where everyone's lives were intertwined, no one wanted to be gossiped about by the neighbors.

One Negro woman, in describing her loneliness up North, said that in the South she was always helping people through her church, but when she came north she didn't do that kind of work any more because she didn't really feel part of her city church. "It's too large," she said. "It just don't see the small people." She added that the preacher didn't even know her name.

Negroes who migrated north were cut off from the warmth and security of community ties. Group controls dissolved as the migrants drifted about in the large cities and were exposed to all the temptations, diversity and confusion of city life.

In this respect, the Negroes were like many European immigrants who found it hard to adjust to the hustle of city living after having grown up in rural surroundings.

But the Negroes faced much greater hostility because of

their color and the stigma attached to their history as slaves. While they were treated better in the North—where they had more legal rights, were not lynched by mobs, were not segregated by state laws and could vote—they were still regarded as inferiors who had to "keep their place." Bigotry was almost as strong in the North as in the South; it was just practiced in different, more subtle ways, with less terror.

Nevertheless, the comparative freedom, and especially the freedom from fear, was a new experience for American Negroes. A black man could feel "more like a man," and could assert himself more up North. This alone nourished greater feelings of self-esteem and stimulated the long-suppressed desire for true equality. More often now, attempts to keep the Negro "in his place" were met with an angry resistance born out of newly awakened pride.

Under such circumstances, and with so many Negroes pouring into the North so quickly, racial friction was inevitable. It finally burst out into the open during the "red summer" of 1919, when a wave of bloody race riots swept across the Northern cities. Stemming partly from the Northern whites' fear of and resistance to the Negro, as well as the Negroes' frustration and disillusionment with life in "the promised land," the riots took many lives. Southern cities, too, were torn apart, so that by the end of the year, America had been wracked by more than 25 race riots. Among the worst were the eruptions in Chicago; Washington, D.C.; Omaha, Nebraska; Longview, Texas; Knoxville, Tennessee; and Elaine, Arkansas.

The immediate cause of each varied. In Chicago, when a young Negro boy swam across an imaginary "color line" and landed on the white side of a public beach, it touched off a five-day riot in which 15 whites and 23 Negroes were killed. A total of 518 persons were injured. The Washington,

Omaha and Knoxville riots stemmed from charges that Negroes had tried to attack white women.

In Longview, a group of white men invaded a Negro section to search for a black school teacher who had reported a lynching to the *Chicago Defender*. The white men were killed by a group of Negroes who were defending the teacher, and a race riot ensued.

In Elaine, a deputy sheriff was killed when he and a posse tried to break up a meeting of Negro farm workers who were organizing to prevent their landlords from cheating them. This set off another riot.

Altogether, several hundred Negroes and whites were killed during the 1919 race riots. The violence snuffed out the "migration fever," although the northward movement kept up at a slow pace throughout the 1920s. By 1929, more than one million Negroes had left their Southern farms to settle in the large urban centers of the North. Although they had experienced many disappointments with their new life, they had at least gained a foothold in American industry and were enjoying some benefits of the nationwide prosperity.

Then the Depression struck.

Factories, mills and shops shut down, and millions of Americans were thrown out of work. Though times were bad for whites, they were far worse for blacks. Negroes were the first to be fired and the last to be hired, so that their economic gains were completely wiped out. The lowest-level jobs were taken over by desperate whites. Negroes were still stuck at the bottom of the ladder, only the bottom was lower than it had ever been before.

Although there was little work for Negroes, or anyone, in the North during the 1930s, conditions in the South were no better. Hoping at least to escape the brutal racial oppression, Negroes continued to migrate North at a steady pace despite the shortage of jobs. About 400,000 rural Negroes moved to the Northern cities during the Depression years.

The discrimination they found there was of a different nature, but equally soul-shattering. In his autobiography, the late Black Muslim leader Malcolm X told what life was like for a Negro boy growing up in Michigan during the 1930s.

On the surface, he said, everything was fine. As the only Negro boy in his class at Mason Junior High School, he was unique, "like a pink poodle." He was popular with the other students, his grades were among the best in the school and he was in demand at basketball games and other school activities. He was even elected class president in the seventh grade.

"And I was proud," he wrote, "I'm not going to say I wasn't. In fact, by then I really didn't have much feeling about being a Negro, because I was trying so hard, in every way I could, to be white."

But the reality of his second-class status hit him one afternoon while he was having a friendly talk with one of his favorite teachers, Mr. Ostrowski.

"Malcolm, you ought to be thinking about a career," Mr. Ostrowski said. "Have you been giving it thought?"

"Well, yes, sir," said Malcolm. "I've been thinking I'd like to be a lawyer."

"Mr. Ostrowski looked surprised, I remember," Malcolm X wrote, "and leaned back in his chair and clasped his hands behind his head. He kind of half-smiled and said, 'Malcolm, one of life's first needs is for us to be realistic. Don't misunderstand me now. We all here like you, you know that. But you've got to be realistic about being a nigger. A lawyer—that's no realistic goal for a nigger. You need to think about something you *can* be. You're good with your hands—making things. Everybody admires your carpentry shop work. Why

don't you plan on carpentry? People like you as a person—
you'd get all kinds of work.' "

Negroes were simply not expected to have higher ambitions. As Malcolm X wrote, "I know that he probably meant
well in what he happened to advise me that day. I doubt that
he meant any harm. It was just in his nature as an American
white man. I was one of his top students, one of the school's
top students—but all he could see for me was the kind of
future 'in your place' that almost all white people see for
black people."

By 1940, the Negro population in the Northern cities had
risen to about four million. It had more than doubled in the
30 years since 1910. But two-thirds of all American Negroes
still lived on the farms and in the towns and villages of the
Old Confederacy. The tidal wave was yet to come.

The second mass migration, which started during World
War II, totally dwarfed the earlier one. The war pulled the
country out of its economic slump. Industries were operating at full blast to turn out all the goods needed for the war
effort. With 10 million men in uniform, labor was in desperate demand and wages were high. Negroes found plenty of
well-paying jobs on the assembly lines in Detroit, where they
were producing tanks and jeeps in place of automobiles.
Shipyards, steel mills and aircraft plants drew Negro workers
to places like Oakland, California; Camden, New Jersey; New
York City; Pittsburgh, Pennsylvania; Gary, Indiana; and
Chicago.

The business boom continued into the postwar years, as
manufacturers once again turned their attention to producing
consumer goods. The automobile companies, seeking unskilled workers for their assembly lines, sent agents down
South to recruit Negro laborers.

But actually, very little recruiting was needed, for many rural Negroes were out of work and desperate for jobs. In the South, and elsewhere throughout the country, millions of farm workers were being forced off the land as the mechanization of agriculture accelerated at a frenzied pace. The trend that had started in the previous century was coming to full maturity in the postwar decades, with startling results.

The small family farm practically became extinct as those who could not afford the new machinery were unable to compete. Farming was big business now, as farm machinery advanced to the point where few people were needed to run a large-scale, modern farm.

Today, it is estimated that only 5 per cent of the American people are still living and working on farms, although the rural population as a whole is about 30 per cent. Furthermore, the 5 per cent can produce such huge quantities of food that for years the federal government has been paying farmers *not* to grow so much. This is a long way from the days of Thomas Jefferson, when 90 per cent of the people were needed on the land to produce the nation's food supply.

The deep South was among the last sections of the country to become highly mechanized. But once the machines did come in, both the Negroes and the poorer white farmers were hard hit. In just 10 years, from 1950-60, almost 6½ million Southerners moved from rural to urban areas. Of these, 4½ million were white and 2 million were Negro.

For the most part, the whites settled in Southern cities, monopolizing all the jobs that were available. The dispossessed Negroes couldn't find any work at all in the Southern cities, so they headed north.

Almost every major Northern city recorded a huge gain in its Negro population over the postwar decades, as the number of blacks in the North more than tripled. Between 1940 and 1960, New York's Negro population increased 2½ times to 14 per cent of the total; in Chicago, Negroes had grown to 24 per cent of the population; in Philadelphia, the figure was 26 per cent; in Detroit, it reached 29 per cent; and in Newark, it climbed to 34.4 per cent.

These percentages continued to soar during the 1960s, so that today all of them are much higher. Negroes now form a majority of the population in Newark, as well as in Washington, D.C., and Gary, Indiana. It is expected that by 1984, 11 more cities will have black majorities, including Chicago, Philadelphia and Detroit.

These gains are not coming from migration alone. The Negro birth rate has been higher than that of whites. Also, large numbers of whites have been moving out of the central cities, leaving behind a higher proportion of blacks.

But whatever the cause, the explosive population growth of Negroes has created a tremendous social upheaval in Northern urban areas. No other ethnic group has ever grown so rapidly or soared to such a high percentage of the population of major American cities. Hundreds of smaller Northern cities have also been affected, including Rochester and Buffalo, New York; Toledo and Akron, Ohio; New Haven, Connecticut; Fort Wayne, Indiana; Milwaukee, Wisconsin; Kansas City, Missouri; and Wichita, Kansas.

What makes the situation critical is that Negroes have been trapped in an economic squeeze. On the one hand, they were dispossessed from the land and driven up North to search for work. But there was little work for them. Northern industry was going through its own technological revolution, and millions of unskilled laborers were being replaced by automatic machinery.

Negro workers, coming up from the rural South, were mainly unskilled and poorly educated. Other immigrant groups before them—equally unskilled and uneducated—had come to the urban centers at a time when unskilled labor was sorely needed. A strong back and a willingness to work were the major requirements in factories, mines, railroads, etc. It didn't matter much whether a man had gone to school or could read and write. Most immigrants had got their start doing this type of unskilled labor, and worked themselves up from there.

But by the time the majority of Negroes migrated to the cities, there wasn't much need for that kind of work. The demand was for white-collar workers or people with vocational training and skills. Most Negroes were not qualified—and even when they were, white labor unions wouldn't let them in and white employers wouldn't hire them.

The result was that they couldn't find jobs. The work that was open to them was so menial, and paid so little compared to what most people were making, that they could scarcely get along on it.

Large numbers of urban Negroes wound up on the cities' welfare rolls at a time when most Americans were prospering. To be poor in a country where most people are poor is bad enough. But to be poor when the great majority are well-off is a crushing experience that does great psychological damage.

Negroes were crowded into filthy, rat-infested slums that rapidly grew larger. As they overflowed into previously all-white neighborhoods, racial friction arose, frequently erupting in brutal gang fights among teen-agers and other forms of violence. Neighborhoods changed quickly from all white to all black, so that larger and larger sections of major cities became ghetto slums.

Mainly as a result of residential patterns, Negro children frequently wound up in all-black schools. They were not being segregated by law, but the effect was pretty much the same. The black schools were overcrowded and poorly staffed, and many white teachers made no attempt to hide their distaste for their black pupils.

Truancy figures rose. Many black youngsters dropped out of school at the earliest possible age, barely able to read and write, and untrained for any occupation. Many of them had grown up on welfare, and as adults they became second-generation welfare recipients. The poverty cycle was perpetuating itself.

Drug addiction among the young soared to alarming heights. So did the crime rate in the major cities. Vice and corruption flourished openly on the ghetto streets.

Negroes had come North to escape poverty and oppression. Once they were there, they had no more illusions—only bitterness and despair. For as Claude Brown said, "Where does one run to when he's already in the promised land?"

9

THE FLIGHT TO SUBURBIA

At the same time that Negroes were streaming into the cities, middle-class whites began moving out to the suburbs. These two movements were not related to each other at first, but after a while the soaring numbers of poor blacks in the central cities became an added reason for the flight of the white middle class.

"Suburban fever" struck right after World War II ended. Millions of soldiers were returning home to their wives or sweethearts, only to find that there was no place for them to live. America was in the midst of a desperate housing shortage.

During the war, production effects, materials and supplies had been diverted to military needs rather than civilian ones. Few new houses had gone up anywhere, but the shortage was not really felt until all the veterans started coming back from overseas.

In the large cities, the crisis was acute. Rents shot up, so that young couples with children were forced to squeeze into very cramped quarters or double up with parents. If a couple heard about a vacant apartment at a reasonable rent, they would be sure to find a whole line of rival apartment hunters waiting there, too.

This was the situation shortly after the war when the building firm of Levitt & Sons announced that it was putting up a development of several thousand low-cost homes in a Long Island suburb of New York City.

The day the houses went on sale, a mob of thousands nearly broke down the doors of the company. People had started lining up two days ahead of time. The houses were sold out almost at once, sight unseen, from building plans alone.

The houses were priced at $7,990, including some of the major appliances. Although the houses were all alike and none had moie than two bedrooms and an unfinished dormer, they were still an excellent buy for the money at the time.

Levitt was able to do this because of a mass-production system he had developed during the war to provide housing for military personnel. Once the war ended, he used the same techniques to build inexpensive private housing. Other builders rushed to follow his lead.

This was a dramatic departure from prewar times, when private homes were custom-built and fairly expensive. Then only comfortable middle-class or wealthy people could afford suburban houses. But as soon as mass-production techniques were applied to housing, even working-class or lower-middle-class families could afford a small home in the suburbs.

The federal government also helped out. Returning veterans were able to get long-term, low-interest mortgages through the Federal Housing Administration, with almost no down payment.

As a result of all these things, low-cost suburban housing developments sprang up all over the country. Homes were built for almost every income group, and even if most of them lacked style or individuality, they still provided more space than most apartment dwellers had had before.

In addition, owning a home had always been at the core of the "American dream." It was part of the country's rural tradition, which extolled the simple virtues of country living as opposed to the frenzy of city life.

Suburbia was not exactly rural, but it was far different from living in a rented apartment in an overcrowded city. For one thing, when people bought a home, it was theirs—they were not paying rent to some landlord.

Second, they were buying a piece of land they could call their own—even if it was only postage-stamp size—and this, too, was part of the rural heritage. Mowing the lawn and planting shrubs on a Saturday afternoon did not exactly constitute a "back to nature" movement, but people were closer to the land than in a rented third-floor walk-up.

For those who had grown up in cities, with few places to play other than the congested streets, the idea of grass and trees and a private back yard seemed like the ultimate in good living. Most young couples wanted these benefits for their children, so they were irresistibly drawn to the suburbs.

The majority of Americans had lived in cities by necessity rather than choice, anyhow. They had gone where the best jobs and business opportunities were, and as the nation became increasingly industrialized, they had little choice but to live in urban areas.

However, the automobile freed people from the necessity of living close to where they worked. When Henry Ford brought the automobile within reach of average American families, he also made suburban living possible for them. Of course, it was a number of years before there were enough good roads and gas stations to make cars practical for everyday use, and by that time the Depression had reduced people's incomes so that they could not afford to buy or maintain a car, let alone a house.

However, after World War II, the economy was thriving once again. The 1950s and 1960s were a boom period for most Americans. They were earning more money and living better than ever before. As a whole, the new generation of young adults were better educated than their parents; they had higher ambitions and wanted more of the good things in life than previous generations even dared to dream of.

The trend among this generation was to move away from the cities—away from the congestion, noise, traffic, crime and other city problems; away, too, from the growing numbers of urban blacks who were fanning out into previously all-white neighborhoods.

Negroes did not share in this move towards suburbia. For the most part, they didn't have the money. Although the country as a whole was prospering, Negroes still had only a small share of the economic pie. They, too, were better off than in previous times, but their standard of living was not rising as fast as the whites'. This meant that the income gap between rich and poor, white and black, was actually getting larger.

Even middle-class Negroes found it extremely difficult to buy a house in the suburbs because the color barrier was as strong as the financial barrier. When the first black family bought a home in the suburban development of Levittown, Pennsylvania, a near-riot ensued. Five hundred angry white homeowners confronted the Negro family the day they moved in. The mob shouted obscenities and hurled stones. Local police were either unable or unwilling to restore order, so the state police had to be called in.

Most builders of suburban developments would not sell to Negroes for fear their presence would drive away white purchasers. This was true even in states that had antidiscrimination laws.

When Levitt & Sons built a low-cost housing development in Willingboro Township (Levittown), New Jersey, in 1958, the firm openly announced that it would not sell houses to Negroes—despite the state law that forbade discrimination in housing supported by federal subsidies. (The Federal Housing Administration supplied mortgage insurance on Levitt houses, which meant that Levittown was federally subsidized in an indirect way.)

Two Negroes who had been denied houses in the development took their case to court. Levitt decided to fight the suit at first. During two years of legal maneuvering the majority of houses in Levittown were sold only to white families. By 1960, when it was clear that Levitt would lose the case, he announced that he would desegregate the remaining sections of the development voluntarily.

Integration was accomplished peacefully, with little open hostility from the white residents. Care was taken to see that Negroes were scattered throughout the community, rather than being grouped together in one area.

Even so, by 1964, Levittown, New Jersey, was less than 1 per cent black. Although the houses were inexpensive—ranging from $11,500 to $14,500, with a down payment of just $100—this was still more than many Negroes could afford. Also, black families were reluctant to move into an overwhelmingly white area, where they might feel lonely and left out.

What was true in the low-priced developments like Levittown was doubly true in the higher-priced suburban communities. There are few, if any, Negroes in the more affluent suburban housing developments across the country. Although there may be separate small, black neighborhoods in many suburban towns, the white and black communities usually have little contact with each other.

The spread of suburbia has cut deeply into America's remaining countryside. There is not very much land left now that can really be called "rural," for much of it has been engulfed by the suburban sprawl.

The Levittown in New Jersey, for example, used to be a sparsely settled area of small farms where peaches, plums and tomatoes were grown. At that time the region was called Willingboro Township. (It has since been renamed Willingboro.) Even though it was only 17 miles away from Philadelphia, it was rural in character and appearance.

Politically, the area had been dominated by a few families whose ancestors had also been active in community life ever since the township was founded 125 years earlier. One or two of these families were wealthy, but the rest were from the lower middle class.

Their roots went deep into the history of Willingboro Township. They were born and raised there, and so were their parents and grandparents. They went to school there, got married there and went to work there. They all voted Republican, so that local affairs were managed under a one-party system.

After World War II, suburbia reached out towards Willingboro Township, fanning out in an ever-widening ring around Philadelphia. As the inner lands filled up, suburbanites spilled over into the outer regions. Finally, Levitt & Sons bought up a huge tract of land in outlying Willingboro, put up 12,000 homes and changed a rural area into a suburban one. A thorough study of this new suburb was made by the sociologist Herbert J. Gans, in his book *The Levittowners*.

Dr. Gans actually bought a home in the development and lived there while observing it.

The people who bought the Levitt homes had no roots in the area. Many were from Philadelphia or other parts of Pennsylvania and New Jersey; many were transients who were being moved about by the Army, others were from scattered corners of the country who had come to the Northeast because of their jobs. Although most of the newcomers intended to settle in these homes permanently, others expected to move elsewhere in a few years.

None of these people worked in the township. Their jobs were mainly in Philadelphia or nearby Camden, New Jersey, and they commuted back and forth. In this sense, they were city-oriented people rather than rural people, for they didn't depend on the town or each other for their livelihoods. This is one of the fundamental differences between a suburban community and a rural town, where people work as well as live.

The newcomers far outnumbered the older residents, and displaced them as community leaders after the first few years —upsetting traditions that had endured for more than a century.

For one thing, they introduced a two-party system in local elections, with Democrats and Republicans battling over such issues as taxes, zoning and parking regulations. In 1959, the Democrats won; in 1960, it was the Republicans' turn for victory; in 1961, the Democrats were back in power; but in 1962, the Republicans won again. Neither group could establish a clear majority.

Second, the newcomers brought religious diversity. The area had been entirely Protestant, but only 47 per cent of the Levittowners were of that faith. Of the rest, 37 per cent were Catholic, 14 per cent were Jewish and the remainder had no religious ties. The Catholics and Jews built their own houses of worship almost at once, for none existed for them in the area.

But most of the friction between the Levittowners and the rural people centered around the school system. The superintendent of schools was a local man who had grown up in the area and gone to the same schools he now supervised. His educational values were mainly rural, lower-middle-class and anti-intellectual. He went out of his way to avoid hiring teachers from large cities, particularly those who leaned towards progressive education.

His most important concern was reading, but he did not believe children should read above their own grade level. For example, in interviewing prospective teachers, he always asked them what they would do if a third-grade pupil had finished his third-grade reader before the end of the term. If the teacher said she would give the child a fourth-grade reader, she was *not* hired. The superintendent felt that such a pupil should be given a supplementary third-grade reader, rather than going on to fourth-grade work.

Similarly, he was most interested in average students, slow learners or the retarded, so that any special programs were devoted to their needs. Bright students were lowest on his list of priorities—partly because he felt they needed less help and partly because he didn't like their behavior or their anxious concern with college scholarships.

He felt that if the curriculum stressed college preparatory work, the average students would be neglected. He also rejected such ideas as teaching foreign languages in elementary schools or letting bright pupils skip to a higher grade. He stressed athletics and practical subjects, such as typing.

Basically, he also seemed to feel that most of his new students were "foreigners," and that it was his duty to "Americanize" them through the school system. His previous, rural-bred students were descended mainly from early colonial stock, so even though the Levittown pupils were third- and fourth-generation Americans, they may have seemed "foreign" by comparison.

The superintendent of schools and the Levittown parents did not get along well at all. Even though a relatively small number of parents were anxious to get their children into "name" colleges, they were a very vocal and forceful group. They wanted to push their children ahead as fast as possible. Their concern started at the kindergarten level and grew more intense as their children got closer to college age.

These parents were engaged in many disputes with the school superintendent, and by 1962 they had mustered enough strength within the community to force his resignation. The type of education that had satisfied the rural families of Willingboro Township did not meet the needs of the suburbanites, who had different goals for their children.

Thus, in education, politics and religious diversity, a rural area was transformed into a suburban one in just a few short years. The same thing was happening throughout the nation as people brought their city habits and attitudes with them into once-rural areas.

Although many people have been fleeing to suburbia to escape city problems, some of these problems have been catching up with them in recent years. Many industries have spread out to the suburbs, bringing needed tax dollars but polluting the air and water as well. Traffic jams extend far out onto the highways and expressways that suburban commuters must use to reach their city jobs.

But perhaps the most critical problems have involved suburban teen-agers. Most suburbs were not designed with teen-agers in mind. These youngsters are at an age where they crave freedom to get about by themselves, plenty of activity and places where they can meet and just "hang around." But in suburbia, they can't get around without a car. Bus transportation is usually so poor that they must depend on their parents or neighbors to drive them places, at least until they are old enough to drive by themselves. Although their parents may have moved to the suburbs so their children could have a better start in life, many suburban adolescents complain loudly about being "bored" and having "nothing to do."

The problem of teen-age drug addiction—once confined mainly to the slum neighborhoods of the cities—has now spread to the suburbs. Growing numbers of middle-class suburban youngsters have been experimenting with a great variety of drugs. Although middle-class teen-agers tend to shy away from "hard stuff"—addictive drugs like heroin and cocaine—they do play around with marijuana, hashish, LSD and "speed" (methedrine).

It was problems such as these that drove people out of the cities in the first place. But even though the suburbs are not trouble-free, the problems there exist on a much smaller scale. Drug addiction in suburbia does not even compare with the very high addiction rate in the cities. There is far less crime in the suburbs, and almost none of the muggings and other street crimes that have made the cities so unsafe.

Although poverty certainly exists in the suburbs, it also appears on a much smaller scale. Suburbanites can generally ignore the small, poor, run-down neighborhood several miles away, while city dwellers bump into the poor almost every time they turn a corner.

More often than not, these urban poor are also black, and they are part of what white Americans are trying to escape when they move to the suburbs. As far back as 1961, the

United States Commission on Human Rights reported: "There is an ever-increasing concentration of nonwhites in racial ghettos, largely in the decaying centers of our cities— while a 'white noose' of new suburban housing grows up around them."

This pattern accelerated rapidly throughout the 1960s, with the suburbs growing five times as fast as the central cities. In 1960, the total number of suburbanites was about 50 million. By 1965, it had climbed to more than 60 million. More and more middle-class whites have been heading for the outer reaches of suburbia and turning their backs on the decaying cities. Left behind are growing numbers of urban blacks—still poor, more frustrated and increasingly angry.

10

THE NEW POWER
STRUGGLE

On a hot summer day in 1964, a scuffle broke out on the streets of Yorkville, in an expensive area near midtown Manhattan. During the melee, an off-duty white police lieutenant shot and killed a 15-year-old Negro boy.

The incident drew angry protests from black groups throughout the city, who accused the policeman of being "trigger-happy" and of killing the boy without just cause. Two nights later, workers from the Congress of Racial Equality, one of the leading black civil rights organizations, held a protest rally on the crowded streets of Harlem. For a speaker's platform, they set up a kitchen chair decorated with a small American flag. Speaker after speaker climbed onto the chair to protest the shooting incident and cry out against police brutality toward blacks.

A large crowd of Negroes gathered around the makeshift platform, growing angrier as the night wore on. Finally, the crowd formed a procession and marched to the nearest police station to demand the arrest of the lieutenant.

As the police tried to hold back the mob, fighting broke out. Sixteen demonstrators were seized by the police, pulled inside the station house and arrested. Then the police tried to clear the street by pushing the other demonstrators back. They used their billy sticks. The mob fought back with bricks and bottles—and soon all of Harlem erupted.

Gangs of black youths raced up and down the streets, smashing windows, looting stores, overturning cars and setting fires. Harlem was sealed off as police tried to contain the rioters.

Disturbances continued for several days, but by the time Harlem cooled down, Brooklyn's huge black Bedford-Stuyvesant ghetto had exploded. The riot followed the same pattern of vandalism, looting and arson. When it was all over, one person had died, 141 were injured and 519 were in jail.

The New York City riots had barely ended when new racial turmoil broke out 200 miles upstate in the city of Rochester. This had begun over a very minor incident—a policeman had tried to arrest a drunken boy at a dance. Four days of wanton rioting followed, during which Governor Nelson Rockefeller sent National Guard troops into the city. The toll in this riot was four dead, 350 wounded and 973 arrested.

The following summer, in the black section of Watts in Los Angeles, a state trooper stopped a Negro youth for drunken driving. The boy's mother arrived on the scene and began arguing with the trooper. A crowd gathered, and behind them more police. Shouts and insults were exchanged. Suddenly rocks started flying, and another race riot had begun.

"Burn, baby, burn!" was the chant among rioting blacks as nearly all of Watts was reduced to ashes and rubble. Stores that were owned by Negroes, and identified by hastily scrawled signs saying "Soul Brother" or "Blood Brother," were usually spared by the rioters.

When the noted civil rights leader the late Martin Luther King, Jr., came to Watts to try to halt the rioting, the mobs mocked and jeered him. Black comedian Dick Gregory also tried to cool tempers. At one point, he walked down a street by himself, imploring rioters to go home. Someone from the crowd fired at him, wounding him in the thigh. Gregory reeled for a moment, then went over to the assailant with the rifle. "You shot me once," he shouted "Now get off the Goddamn street!"

But such efforts were of little use. A "state of insurrection" was proclaimed in Watts as the fighting spread over 24 square miles of southern Los Angeles. Fifteen thousand national guardsmen were called in to quell the violence, and when it was over, the devastation was terrible. Thirty-six people were dead, more than 900 were injured and 4,000 were jailed. The damage was estimated at about $200 million, with 209 businesses totally destroyed and 787 partly destroyed.

The violence in Watts shook up the nation far more than the race riots of the previous summer. For one thing, Watts didn't even look much like a slum ghetto. It was hard for white Americans to understand why so much rage had poured out of this neat-looking neighborhood where rows of one- and two-story homes were set back on grassy lawns. These houses looked nothing like the crumbling, overcrowded tenements of Harlem, where poverty and misery were so plainly seen. Also, the incident that had touched off all this destruction was just a minor, everyday traffic arrest.

New riots followed this pattern, as the urban ghettos became tinderboxes during the hot summer of 1966. On a sweltering day in Chicago, when the temperature had soared to 95 degrees, ghetto youngsters were cooling themselves at an open water hydrant. The police came and turned off the hydrant—igniting a three-day riot in which two people were killed and 83 wounded.

On another hot night in the black Hough district of Cleveland, a Negro man walked into a white-owned tavern and asked for a glass of ice water. When the bartender refused to give him one, he went outside and complained loudly to the people on the street. A crowd formed, and within minutes they had stormed the bar and wrecked it. This was the start of a week-long riot in which four were killed and 46 injured.

The summer of 1967 was shattered by two furious riots—one in Newark, New Jersey, where conditions in the black ghetto were among the worst anywhere, and one in Detroit, where conditions were among the best. Ironically, the Detroit riot was the most destructive of them all, claiming 40 lives and causing about $1 billion in damage.

Typically, it started with a routine police action. At about 4 A.M. one morning, police raided a west side, ghetto-area "blind pig"—an after-hours speakeasy. They arrested about 80 persons, and brought them outside to patrol wagons. A crowd gathered, some rocks were thrown and then someone made a direct hit, smashing the window of a police car. As if by signal, the mob suddenly went wild and the riot was on.

For five days, Detroit blazed with hundreds of fires. Nothing was spared as mobs ravaged "Soul Brother" shops as well as stores owned by whites. For the first time in a quarter of a century, federal troops were sent into a Northern city to put down the riot. Detroit looked like a war zone, as tanks rolled through the streets and United States soldiers stood guard with machine guns or patrolled the city with rifles and bayonets.

At the end, more than 2,000 people were injured and another 2,500 were left homeless. Arrests climbed to over 4,000.

The race-riot epidemic reached its peak during the summer of 1967, as more than 50 cities in addition to Detroit and

Newark were plagued by racial violence. During the four summers of turmoil that had begun with the Harlem riot in 1964, cities from coast to coast had been affected. These included places like Omaha, Nebraska; Minneapolis, Minnesota; Philadelphia; Providence, Rhode Island; Perth Amboy, New Jersey; Atlanta, Georgia; Dayton, Ohio; and Waukegan, Illinois.

After more fiery upheavals the following spring, in Washington, D.C., Chicago and elsewhere, there were no more major race riots. The fires seemed to have burned themselves out for the time being.

White Americans and middle-class and moderate black Americans were frightened and bewildered by the ferocity of the racial outbursts. Moderate black leaders like Roy Wilkins, of the National Association for the Advancement of Colored People, and Whitney Young, of the Urban League, feared the riots would create an angry "white backlash" that would wipe out all the recent gains Negroes had made in the struggle to secure their rights.

Whites couldn't understand why Negroes should be rioting just when they seemed to be making more progress than ever before. Since 1954, when the Supreme Court first declared segregated schools unconstitutional, true racial equality had seemed to be just around the corner.

Blacks and liberal whites had optimistically joined forces in a nationwide civil rights movement. In the South, there were lunch-counter sit-ins, freedom rides, bus boycotts and other nonviolent demonstrations that challenged the "Jim Crow" segregation laws. One by one, the Supreme Court was striking down these laws and removing any legal basis for segregation.

In the North, where there was racial imbalance in the

schools because of residential patterns rather than laws, civil rights leaders had been working out plans to bus black children to white schools and vice versa. Although there was strong opposition to these plans, the first few were being put into effect.

There were new federal civil rights laws, too—the first since Reconstruction times. They protected Negroes against discrimination in such places as hotels, motels, restaurants and theaters. Discrimination by unions and employers in certain industries was also banned by law. In addition, Congress passed a Voting Rights Act to protect Negroes from disenfranchisement. Negroes had been pressing for such federal bills for years.

The goals of the civil rights movement were to end all forms of discrimination and to achieve integration in schools, housing and jobs. It was believed that only in a fully integrated society could blacks have the same opportunities to succeed as whites.

As one Negro mother said: "If my child sits next to a white child in school, it doesn't guarantee that she will learn—but it does guarantee that she will at least be *taught*."

Just when Negroes seemed to be on the verge of achieving these goals through the law courts, the race riots began—and the nation demanded to know why.

The answer came as a shock.

After carefully examining the nature of the riots, the 11-man National Advisory Committee on Civil Disorders reported that the "fundamental" cause of the rioting was *white racism*, rather than black irresponsibility.

Their study showed that, despite long years of civil rights agitation and many legal victories, Negroes were still being held down by a society that discriminated against them. In both the North and the South, employers, labor unions, landlords and the police were among the many groups guilty of discriminatory practices.

In fact, the dollar gap between white incomes and black incomes had actually increased. According to a joint report of the Commerce and Labor Departments, the 1947 median income of black families had been only $944 less than that of white families. But by 1968, the gap had grown to $3,577. White families were earning an average of $8,936, but the median black family income was $5,359.

Although both groups had made big financial gains in the boom years since 1947, the gains were unequal—leaving Negroes poorer in relation to whites.

In addition, integration was proceeding very slowly, bogged down in long, drawn-out court battles, municipal red tape and other forms of delay. Hopes for true equality, which had been spawned in 1954 by the school desegregation decision, were still far from being realized. Negroes had been expecting great changes in their lives for over a decade—and few had occurred.

Historically, revolutions do not occur when people are most oppressed, but when the lid of oppression has been lifted just enough to rekindle the spirit and arouse hopes for a better future. When these newly aroused hopes are not fulfilled, or the changes come too slowly, people are most likely to turn to violence.

The race riots of 1919 also came at a time when Negroes seemed to be making great strides, but the strides did not nearly match their expectations.

So it was in the 1960s. After years of waiting for something to happen, Negroes were still at the bottom of the ladder in every way. Their standard of living remained far below that of white Americans, even though it was an era of great prosperity.

In Watts, the wide streets and neat rows of houses belied a numbing poverty. Almost one-quarter of the black families there had incomes below the 1965 poverty line of $3,000 per year; more than one-half of them were on relief, and 34 per cent were jobless. Those who had jobs worked mainly as menials—maids, janitors, porters and dishwashers. Only one in ten held a white-collar job.

The social conditions were also appalling. One-third of all youngsters in Watts came from broken homes, and more than one-half were school dropouts. The crime rate was almost twice the average for the city as a whole.

In Harlem, the statistics were very much the same. The unemployment rate among Negroes in the city was double that of whites. One out of four were jobless, and the average income among Negro families was $3,480, compared to the 1964 citywide average of $5,103.

One-quarter of a million black people were jammed into Harlem's 3½ square miles, paying anywhere from $50 to $74 even for one-room flats. Only one-half of all the children in central Harlem lived with their parents, and more than half were high school dropouts. The homicide rate was six times higher than the rest of the city; there was twice as much juvenile delinquency, and ten times as much drug addiction.

The Hough district of Cleveland—also known as "the jungle"—was a rat-infested, garbage-strewn ghetto housing more than 60,000 blacks in two square miles.

Conditions among Negroes in Newark were probably the worst of all. That city was known to have the worst housing, the worst crime rate and the highest rate of venereal disease anywhere in the country.

These kinds of conditions were commonplace in almost every Negro section in every American city. Although growing numbers of middle-class Negroes had broken away from the slums, they were still a relatively small group. Most Negroes were still poor and were still trapped in the decaying ghettos of the inner cities.

The terrible conditions under which they lived, the frustration of their hopes and their rising anger were all packed into the violent eruptions that rocked American cities for four summers. This rage also led to the rise of a new group of black leaders who were younger and far more militant than the old Negro leadership.

Men like the late Malcolm X, Stokely Carmichael, H. Rap Brown, Eldridge Cleaver and Huey Newton began to challenge both the methods and the goals of the older civil rights movement. For one thing, they did not reject violence as a means of achieving their aims. They argued that when an oppressed group could not secure its rights peacefully, it was justified in using violence—just as the American colonists did when England did not grant them their rights.

These militant young spokesmen also rejected integration as a primary goal, emphasizing various forms of "black power" or "black separatism" instead. This meant that, instead of trying to break up the ghettos to integrate American society, they wanted to develop black economic and political strength *within* the ghettos.

According to the "black power manifesto" formulated by Stokely Carmichael, former chairman of the Student Nonviolent Coordinating Committee: "If we are to proceed toward liberation, we must cut ourselves off from white people. We must form our own institutions, credit unions, co-ops, political parties, and write our own histories."

If this was the official definition of "black power," it had different meanings for different people. Some thought it preached race hatred of whites; others regarded it as a legitimate demand for economic and political power within the

American system; others thought it advocated a separate black society inside white America but independent from it.

Only one thing was clear: the tone of the new movement was not as patient or as peaceful as the old.

Liberal whites who had been working in the civil rights movement found they were no longer welcome in the more militant organizations, particularly in any sort of leadership role. These groups were going to be run by and for blacks only.

The NAACP, the Urban League and the Southern Christian Leadership Conference refused to go along with the "black power" doctrine because they felt it had overtones of antiwhite racism. These groups still wanted to work with whites towards the full integration of American society.

But the Black Muslims, SNCC and more recent and violent groups like the Black Panthers adopted varying forms of the new doctrine. The Congress of Racial Equality, an older, well-established civil rights group on the level of the NAACP or the Urban League, also came out in favor of "black power." This caused a split in the civil rights movement, with the moderate wing holding out for peaceful integration and the militant wing opting for "black power" and, possibly, violence as a means of achieving it.

Although most Negroes in this country still seem to prefer nonviolence and integration as the best way of gaining equality, the angry young militants have made a smashing impact. There is no doubt that the fear of more violence has spurred efforts by government officials, businessmen and politicans to open up more opportunities for Negroes, particularly in jobs and education.

After the 1965 Watts riot, Vice-President Hubert Humphrey urged businessmen to bring jobs into the area.

One of the first firms to respond was Aerojet-General, a subsidiary of the General Tire and Rubber Company.

In August, 1966, Aerojet set up the Watts Manufacturing Company in the heart of the ghetto. The company had a contract with the federal government to supply $2.5 million worth of tents for the armed forces.

There were 440 job openings, and ghetto residents were hired almost entirely on a "first come" basis. They were not tested for knowledge or skills; the company felt that such tests did not show the real abilities of people who had been so poorly educated that they could not handle a written test. More than 80 per cent of those hired had no real work experience, and more than half had police records.

Many of the new employees had never had the chance to develop disciplined work habits, so the rate of absenteeism was terribly high at first—up to 35 per cent on Monday mornings.

But gradually, people developed pride in their growing skills. Also, the company introduced a piecework incentive system under which ambitious workers could earn up to $25 a day. After a while, absenteeism dropped to about 8 per cent. A number of workers were promoted, and one man who hadn't held a job in five years became a supervisor.

Productivity also shot up. In the beginning, the unskilled, untrained workers could turn out only about one tent a day each. But later on, each employee could finish as many as 22 tents in a single day.

The company expanded, taking on contracts to make metal parts and wooden shipping crates. The number of employees was doubled to about 900, and the company found that it had reached the break-even point much earlier than expected.

The Watts Manufacturing Company is just one small example of what private industry can do to provide work for people in the urban ghettos. On a larger scale is the program under way in Brooklyn's Bedford-Stuyvesant area.

The idea for this program originated in 1964, during the Senatorial campaign of the late Robert F. Kennedy. While Kennedy was touring the Bedford-Stuyvesant area and speaking to residents, he was so appalled by the bleakness, decay and misery he saw that he pledged to help restore the neighborhood by bringing in new businesses and schools.

After his election, he set up the Bedford-Stuyvesant Restoration Corporation, a group that is run by black leaders in the community and is financed mainly by federal grants. This group has succeeded in attracting a number of businesses and industries to Bedford-Stuyvesant, with the understanding that they will employ many neighborhood people. Also, the corporation helps Negroes who want to go into business for themselves in Bedford-Stuyvesant, supplying low-cost loans, legal and technical advice and other services.

A new college of the City University of New York will also be located in Bedford-Stuyvesant as a result of Senator Kennedy's efforts. If original plans are followed, this college will be run on a much more flexible and experimental basis than the other colleges in the city system.

On a nationwide scale is the National Alliance of Businessmen, a group organized by Henry Ford II in 50 major cities across the country. It has been persuading businessmen and industrialists to hire the "hard core" unemployed. These are people who are not just temporarily jobless, but who lack even the basic skills and education needed in today's job market. Many of these people can barely read, have no confidence in their ability to do a job and lack motivation.

Complete training programs are needed before they can even begin to tackle a job. But if firms are willing to hire the hard-core unemployed, they can get grants from the Department of Labor to train them.

For example, under a contract with the Labor Department, the Chrysler Corporation hired and trained 3,000 hard-core unemployed in 1968 to work in six company plants and in car dealerships in 50 cities. The training program lasted 12 weeks. Those who went into Chrysler plants afterwards got assembly-line jobs at about $3.13 an hour.

Such programs are being developed by many firms in cities across the nation in an effort to reduce hard-core unemployment among ghetto residents.

Although in the past Negroes found it hard to get jobs because employers discriminated against them, this has become less of a problem in recent years. Businessmen have shown a growing willingness to hire black workers, particularly the skilled and better educated. However, promotions of Negroes into the upper ranks of businesses is still a rarity.

Perhaps the biggest obstacle to Negro advancement in the last decades has been the white working class. This is the group that has the most to lose, because when Negroes advance up the economic ladder, they will be competing with white workers for the better-paying jobs.

Labor unions, particularly the craft unions, have been excluding all but a handful of Negroes. In this respect, they have been acting as the voice of the white workingman, not the black workingman.

It wasn't too long ago that unions were considered among the most progressive and liberal forces in the nation. They were catalysts for social and political change at a time when the struggle was between capital and labor.

But once the struggle shifted to the area of equal job opportunities for Negroes, the unions were not so eager for reform. If they admitted more Negroes, they would be going against the interests of their white membership. Faced with this inner conflict, most union leaders tried to cling to the status quo.

In New York City, the powerful International Ladies Garment Workers Union came under fierce attack by the NAACP and CORE for its treatment of Negroes. This union was once considered the most militant fighter for social justice in the labor movement. It also became a strong political force in the city through its support of the Liberal Party, which often held the "swing" vote in elections. It was through this union that many Jewish immigrants worked their way up in New York City's garment industry, and the union leadership has always been dominated by Jews.

About 150,000 nonwhite workers belong to the ILGWU, out of a total membership of 450,000. Roy Innis of CORE charged that for years the union has "permitted conditions to exist which keep the vast majority of black workers in the lowest-paying jobs and has denied black workers a policy-making voice in the union through restrictive constitutional provisions."

Similar charges have been hurled at many other industrial unions. But the main target of attack has been the craft unions, particularly in the building trades. Electricians, plumbers, sheet-metal workers and other skilled craftsmen in the building trades are among the highest paid union workers in the country. But until recently, these unions systematically excluded Negroes. As late as 1968, not a single Negro in St. Louis had an Electrical Workers' card that permitted him to work on construction projects.

There are about two million Negroes in organized labor, out of a total membership of about 18 million. Because of discriminatory policies, Negro union members have been concentrated in the lowest-paying and least desirable jobs, including semiskilled trades, menial or service occupations.

But the pressure is on all unions now to open their doors to Negroes and to end discriminatory treatment against black members. This pressure has the force of federal law behind it.

The Civil Rights Act of 1964 banned discrimination by employers or unions in any industry affecting interstate commerce. Since the passage of this act, the NAACP has lodged more than 700 complaints with federal agencies charging union discrimination. Another 1,600 complaints have been filed against employers and employment agencies.

Special pressure has been exerted to open up the construction industry to Negroes. Under the Labor Department's "Philadelphia Plan"—named for the first city in which it was enforced—firms that bid on federal construction projects must promise to hire a specific number of minority-group workers.

Early in 1970, Labor Secretary George P. Shultz announced that the "Philadelphia Plan" would be extended to 18 other cities unless they drew up their own plans for ending job discrimination in the construction industry. Among these cities were Boston, Detroit, Atlanta, Los Angeles, Seattle, Newark, St. Louis and New York.

In addition to their fight for equal job opportunities, Negroes are also battling for more power in other areas. In some cities, "community control" of schools and other neighborhood institutions has become an issue. In New York City, for example, pressure from Negroes resulted in an experiment to decentralize the city's public school system, which had been under the control of one central Board of Education.

The city's schools were in dreadful shape, particularly in Negro and Puerto Rican neighborhoods. They were overcrowded, understaffed and poorly supplied. Teachers found it hard to cope with the ghetto youngsters, whose backgrounds were so different from their own. The pupils did not respond well to the traditional teaching methods, and large numbers were dropping out of the high schools, barely able to read and write.

Also, in many cases, Negro youngsters were being "tracked" into general studies or vocational programs, rather than programs leading to college. The sorting of "bright," "average" and "slow" learners started down near the kindergarten level, so that a child's whole future might be decided for him by the time he was eight or nine.

At first, it was hoped that black children would have a better chance to succeed if the schools were integrated. However, there was such strong opposition to integration plans from white parents that most elementary schools remained heavily imbalanced.

Finally, a number of black community leaders dropped their integration efforts. Instead, they called for a drastic improvement in the existing all-black schools. They wanted neighborhood school boards to have the power to hire and fire teachers, to choose principals and to decide upon the curriculum. Most of all, they wanted more flexibility in the school system so that they could experiment to find the best methods of reaching ghetto youngsters.

As a result of their demands, the city set up two experimental school districts that had a small measure of autonomy, but not nearly as much as black leaders had wanted. When one of the experimental districts apparently overstepped its powers and fired a number of white teachers, the teachers' union went on strike.

For two months, the entire New York City public school system was paralyzed as a result of the power struggle between the union, which was mainly white, and the Negro-led experimental district. An uneasy truce finally ended the strike, but it wasn't long afterwards that the experimental districts were phased out in a new citywide decentralization plan that was more acceptable to the teachers.

In this case, as in so many others, the interests of a union collided with the interests of the black community. This time the union was protecting its members from what it considered unfair and arbitrary dismissals. Such protection is one of the main benefits a union can provide for its members.

On the other hand, the black leaders of the experimental district felt that some teachers were doing a very poor job of educating their youngsters, and they wanted to choose replacements who were more sympathetic to black children's special needs.

Power struggles of this type are certain to increase in every major city as the black populations grow larger and stronger.

Politically, Negroes have made great leaps forward in a number of large cities. In 1967 Cleveland, Ohio, became the first major American city to elect a Negro mayor. Democrat Carl B. Stokes, the great-grandson of a Negro slave, ran for mayor against Republican Seth B. Taft, the grandson of former President William Howard Taft. Stokes won by just 1,644 votes in one of the closest elections in Cleveland's history.

This was Stokes's second try for the mayoralty. Four years earlier he had run as an independent candidate, losing by a small margin. In the intervening years, the city was rocked by race riots in the black Hough district. The terrible conditions there demanded energetic and progressive city action, but little was forthcoming from the men in power.

Stokes challenged the Democratic leadership and entered the primary contest against Mayor Ralph S. Locher. He went on to win the Democratic nomination by about 18,000 votes.

Stokes, a tall, good-looking man with a neat mustache, rose out of the slums himself. His father, a laundry worker, died when Stokes was just a baby. His mother was on relief for a while, and he himself was a high school dropout. But he had always liked to read books, and he used to smuggle them home under his jacket so his friends in the neighborhood wouldn't make fun of him. Reading was not part of the way of life in the ghetto.

He enlisted in the Army, and after his release, he returned to school. In 1954 he graduated from the University of Minnesota, and two years later he got a degree from the Cleveland-Marshall Law School. In 1962, he was elected to the Ohio House of Representatives. He was just 40 years old when he was elected mayor.

Cleveland has a black population of about 300,000 out of a total of 810,000 inhabitants. The whites are divided into many ethnic groups—Poles, Slovaks, Germans, Italians, Czechs and Irish.

Stokes is popular among white voters as well as black. He can soothe a hostile audience with his easy, joking manner, and he is not feared as a radical on civil rights. One of his major projects is "Cleveland NOW," a 10-year, $1.5 billion program to rehabilitate the city with the help of local businessmen and industries.

Another city that elected a Negro mayor in 1967 was Gary, Indiana. Gary, a steel town of mainly blue-collar workers, has a population of about 178,000. Negroes are in the majority, with 55 per cent of the population. However, more whites than blacks are registered voters. In 1964, the white vote in the presidential primary went heavily to George Wallace, the Southern segregationist.

Gary was also known as a very corrupt town, where gambling, prostitution and crooked politics flourished.

In May, 1967, a 34-year-old black attorney named Richard Hatcher entered the Democratic primary for mayor. He was the reform candidate who pledged to end the widespread corruption.

Normally, he could not have won in the tightly controlled city. But this time, two other candidates were in the race. They split the white vote, and Hatcher won the Democratic nomination.

During the campaign, he was practically sabotaged by members of his own party, who had not wanted him at all. At first they cut off his campaign funds so that he lacked the financial support of the Democratic machine.

But after he placed a full-page ad in the *New York Times* appealing for contributions all across the nation, the embarrassed Democratic bosses in Gary restored his funds.

Hatcher conducted a vigorous campaign, particularly in white neighborhoods. When it was over, he had received twelve per cent of the white vote and 95 per cent of the black vote, giving him a narrow victory.

Like Carl Stokes, Hatcher had an impoverished childhood. He was the twelfth of thirteen children. His father was a factory worker who was usually laid off half the year. By means of a church stipend, a small track scholarship and an assortment of odd jobs, Hatcher was able to finance his way through Indiana University. From there he went to Indiana's Valparaiso Law School. In 1963, he was elected to the city council.

Hatcher was battling all the odds in his campaign to become mayor of Gary. Negroes in other cities have also been making political gains, and there are now more black representatives in Congress, state legislatures, city councils and other local boards than ever before. This is true in the South as well as in the North.

But the victories have not come easily. Whether the field of battle is jobs, education or politics, fierce struggles are bound to occur whenever one group is seeking a bigger share of power. As Negroes gain economic and political strength in the cities, the power of the older, established ethnic groups will be diminished. People rarely yield power without a fight, so the cities are bound to face a great deal of turmoil in the years ahead before a new balance of power is reached among competing groups.

11

THE ROTTING CORE

In 1968, the commission appointed by President Johnson to examine the causes of the urban riots reported that America was coming closer and closer to a state of "apartheid"—that is, complete separation of the races.

The commission, headed by Otto Kerner, former Governor of Illinois, stated: "Our nation is moving toward two societies . . . one black, one white, separate and unequal."

In 1969, a similar commission, headed by Milton Eisenhower, did a follow-up study. The results were still more somber. "A year later," the study revealed, "we are a year closer to being two societies, black and white, increasingly separate and scarcely less unequal."

Partly because of antiblack prejudice, whites were leaving the central cities and moving to all-white suburbs, the report stated. Moreover, the white exodus was speeding up as the black migration from rural areas to the cities continued.

If the movement kept up at the same rate, the report predicted, by 1985 the inner cities would have gained 10 million more nonwhites, while the suburbs would have added 53.9 million whites.

This meant that America was becoming more segregated *in fact* at the same time it was becoming less segregated by *law*. It also meant that the inner cities were filling up with more and more poor people.

The outlook for the future of the central cities was very grave. If the process continued, the cities might well become decaying, crime-ridden reservoirs for the poor, while the middle classes—both white and black—lived in outlying suburban areas.

The middle classes have always been the life-sustaining force of the central cities. They owned and occupied most of the housing and maintained it in suitable condition; they owned the many small stores and businesses throughout the cities; their children went to the public schools; they were the solid, stable element of the population that had a big stake in the city, so they used their political and economic power to fight for improvements; and they were the source from which the cities got much of their tax dollars.

As they leave and the poor move into their old neighborhoods, decay sets in. The houses, which by now are older and need more repairs, become expensive to maintain. Absentee landlords tend to let them deteriorate. Single or two-family homes may be turned into rooming houses, packed with more families than they were ever meant to hold.

Poverty and overcrowding result in higher crime rates, which scare away more of the middle class. Old, established neighborhood stores close down, and the blight spreads to the commercial streets. Schools become overcrowded, drug addiction flourishes among the young and the addicts turn to crime to support their habit.

By this process, a stable middle-class neighborhood becomes a slum. Sometimes it happens remarkably fast.

The city no longer gets much tax revenue from the neighborhood because the new residents have low incomes and low buying power. If large numbers of them are unemployed and on welfare, the neighborhood becomes another drain on the city's finances.

Thus, as the middle classes leave, the cities themselves become poorer and less able to finance and equip their schools and transportation systems, their police, fire and sanitation departments, their hospitals and health services and the countless other services that are necessary for the survival of a city.

On the other hand, poor people have a desperate need for *more* public services, like public housing projects and city hospitals, because they cannot afford to pay private rates.

This means that as the city's need for public services grows, its ability to pay for them declines. The money shortage also hinders the cities in their battles against the many other problems that confront them.

Cities have always been plagued with problems of crime, poverty, poor housing, overcrowding and the like. All these things existed long before the large-scale Negro migration from rural to urban areas ever began. But the black migration added the element of racial friction to city life at the same time that the new suburbs were offering an escape from urban problems to all who could afford it.

Today, many cities are in desperate shape. The skyrocketing rate of street crime has begun driving away even those who would normally prefer city to suburban life.

The problem is particularly severe in the nation's capital. In 1969, Washington, D.C., ranked second among American cities in serious crime. In 1968, it had been sixth.

Whites have been leaving the inner city steadily over the last 15 years. More recently, the capital's large Negro middle class has also been leaving the high-crime neighborhoods and heading for the nearby Maryland suburbs of Prince Georges County.

Washington's streets are notoriously unsafe after dark. As President Richard Nixon said in his 1969 State of the Union message: "I doubt if there are many members of this Congress who live more than a few blocks from here who would dare leave their cars in the Capitol Garage and walk home alone tonight."

Just a few hours before he spoke, a major crime had occurred only two blocks from the White House. Three gunmen held up the Commerce Department's federal credit union and escaped with $128,600.

Crime has even spread to the classrooms. For the first time in the city's history, policemen were stationed in all of Washington's 46 junior and senior high schools for an "indefinite" length of time. The city's police force now numbers 4,625— the largest force per capita in any American city.

Those who have moved to the suburbs don't make much use of the city after working hours, seldom visiting its restaurants, shops, theaters and night spots. About 65 per cent of the white suburbanites visit the downtown area less than once a month, and 15 per cent visit less than once a year.

If the crime rate continues to soar, it may drive out the remaining white and black middle class. Those left behind in the nation's capital will be the criminals and their victims—the poor who cannot afford to move away.

Fear of crime is not all that is driving the middle classes out of the cities, although it is becoming more significant every day. Many cities are also facing a severe housing shortage, brought on by the decay and abandonment of old buildings and the failure to replace them with enough good low- or middle-income units. Construction costs have gone up so much in recent years that most new, privately built apartment houses are in the "luxury" class. The number of older, sturdy and less costly buildings is shrinking fast.

In major cities across the country—New York, Detroit, Chicago, Philadelphia, Washington, D.C., New Orleans, Houston and many others—landlords have been abandoning their older buildings rather than investing money in repairs.

Often these buildings could have been put in good shape at reasonable costs, but either they were in "marginal" neighborhoods bordering on high-crime slum areas or in neighborhoods undergoing racial change. White middle-class tenants would not move there, and the poor could not afford rents high enough to cover the cost of the repairs.

Landlords have been letting these buildings deteriorate into rat-infested slum dwellings, or just abandoning them even before they reach that point. Apparently, being a slum landlord is not as profitable as it used to be.

Many blocks in major cities are now filled with abandoned, boarded-up houses or empty shells, giving the areas a bleak, bombed-out appearance. Philadelphia has reported about 24,000 vacant houses, while Houston has about 7,500. In New Orleans, officials closed off a whole section near the center of town because of decay.

In New York City, 33,000 apartments per year were lost between 1965 and 1968 as a result of owner abandonment. This was a loss of nearly 100,000 apartments at a time when there was an acute housing shortage. Rents in the better neighborhoods skyrocketed, so that more and more of the middle class was squeezed out into the suburbs.

Families with young children are affected most by such conditions. They need ample living space at modest prices, and they want the neighborhood streets and playgrounds to be safe for their youngsters. They also want good schools— another factor that has been pushing them towards the suburbs.

In recent years, schools in many cities have been paralyzed by racial unrest, teachers' strikes and student boycotts. Education grinds to a halt during the disruptions, and the resulting tensions and hostility linger for a long time afterwards. The two-month New York City teachers' strike left deep scars, heightening friction between the city's Jewish and Negro populations.

The students, too, were adversely affected. The citywide reading tests given at the end of the school year showed that pupils had fallen two months behind the previous year's achievement levels. Even before the strike, New York's pupils had been below the national average in reading scores.

A study by the Urban Research Corporation of Chicago found that racial tensions were at the core of most school disturbances. From September, 1969, through January, 1970, the study showed that there had been racial incidents in schools in 39 cities. No section of the country was free of serious racial discord in the schools. Furthermore, the unrest had spread from the large cities to the medium-size ones.

Many of the disputes were between white teachers and administrators and black students. But there was also growing animosity between white and black students in integrated schools. In one high school in Detroit, for example, there were a series of fist fights between black and white students. Since then, the two groups have been sitting on opposite sides of the school cafeteria, like two warring camps.

This particular school had undergone rapid racial change. In 1964, more than 90 per cent of the students were white. By 1970, more than half were black. But even in schools where the change was not nearly so dramatic, there has been a growing split among students along racial lines.

Public high schools and even junior high schools in the nation's cities are facing still another grave problem—they have become targets for drug peddlers. Addictive drugs like heroin are being sold to teen-agers in or near the schools, causing an upsurge in deaths among adolescents. In 1964, 38 teen-agers died from the effects of heroin in New York City; in 1969, 224 youngsters died from it. The total number of heroin-caused deaths in New York City that year was 900.

A study by *The New York Times* found that "heroin is probably being sold in almost every public high school in the city, in many junior high schools and in several private and parochial schools. The vast majority of the pushers are students, school-age dropouts or truants.

"Many youthful student pushers have been found to be workers at 'factories' and 'tables' where the heroin is 'cut' and placed in glassine packets. Some even have bought heroin in bulk and set up their own business."

It is estimated that New York City has at least 100,000 drug addicts of whom 25,000 are teen-agers. Since addicts commit nearly half of all the robberies and burglaries in the city to support their habits, a rising crime rate has gone hand in hand with a rising rate of addiction.

The acute problems caused by poverty, racial friction and drug addiction would be bad enough in themselves, but these are only part of what today's cities are faced with.

Traffic congestion in many major cities is appalling. Highways leading to the inner cities from the outlying suburbs are frequently clogged in the morning and evening "rush hours," and the air in the central cities is thick with fumes from automobiles, trucks and buses. Combined with the smoke from factories and houses, this has created serious air pollution problems. Some days it becomes so bad that people in the cities suffer ill effects. Their eyes sting, they wheeze and cough or they develop headaches. Some experts have predicted that if the air pollution keeps getting worse at the same rate, by 1985 the residents of large cities will need gas masks just to survive.

The mass transportation systems of many cities are also in bad shape. Costs have been shooting up rapidly, while service, safety and passenger volume has declined. The number of paying passengers carried by the cities' public and private mass transit systems dropped from 19 billion in 1945 to 6.49 billion in 1968.

Riders are abandoning the buses and subways of the inner cities because of poor service, dirty cars and stations, noise and overcrowding. They have turned to automobiles instead. This has done much to worsen the traffic congestion and increase air pollution.

To make matters worse, fares are going up. In Kansas City, Missouri, bus riders began paying 50¢ a ride in 1970, the highest fare in the country. In Cleveland, fares on city-owned lines have gone up three times since 1960, hitting 35¢ by 1969. The increases were combined with a reduction in service.

Cities must also battle problems of sanitation, overcrowding, noise, high rents, shortages of recreational facilities and rising municipal costs, among many others. Their finances are already being strained to the breaking point, so they cannot adequately provide the many public services that are so vital to city life. That is partly why so many people are moving out.

Various experiments have been undertaken to revive the cities and halt the flight of the middle class. Under President Lyndon Johnson, the emphasis was on physical improvements, such as clearing blighted neighborhoods and putting up low- and middle-income housing. One of his major projects was the Model Cities Program, which was designed to improve the total quality of life in selected neighborhoods through a heavy concentration of federal and local programs.

But President Richard Nixon has de-emphasized these programs. He has been concentrating more on the issue of poverty itself, stressing measures to reform the welfare program, increase employment and feed the hungry.

The problem of poverty is at the very core of the urban crisis. Too many poor people are packed into the central cities, and the middle classes do not want to share the side-effects of poverty with them. They leave, and the cities deteriorate still more.

As President Nixon's study group on urban renewal stated: "There is perhaps no greater danger to the future of our democracy than the possibility that the cities as we have known them will be destroyed as the well-to-do and the white concentrate more and more in the suburbs, with the central cities converted into reservations for the black and the poor."

Diversity has always been the lifeblood of the cities. The great urban centers were shared by people of many different backgrounds, economic classes, ethnic groups, races and religions, each adding bits and pieces of their own culture to the urban mix.

This intermingling of a great variety of people was what made the cities vital and exciting places to live and work. This was what made them the breeding grounds for new ideas, new political and social experiments and new cultural movements.

If the cities are left to become segregated islands of poverty, American civilization as a whole will have lost much of its creative vitality.

SUGGESTED FURTHER READING

1. Allen, Frederick Lewis, *Only Yesterday*, New York: Harper and Row, 1931
2. Burlingame, Roger, *Machines That Built America*, New York: Harcourt, Brace, 1953; also, *March of the Iron Men*, New York: Grosset and Dunlap, 1938
3. Green, Constance McLaughlin, *American Cities in the Growth of the Nation*, New York: Harper and Row, 1965; also, *The Rise of Urban America*, New York: Harper and Row, 1965
4. Kraus, Michael, *Immigration, The American Mosiac*, New Jersey: D. Van Nostrand, 1966
5. Pomerantz, Sidney, *New York, An American City, 1783–1803*, Empire State Historical Publications Ser. No. 27
6. Rattray, Jeanette Edwards, *East Hampton History*, East Hampton, Long Island, 1953 (published privately, copyrighted by Jeanette Rattray)
7. Solomon, Barbara Miller, *Ancestors and Immigrants*, Cambridge, Mass.: Harvard University Press, 1956
8. Turner, Frederick Jackson, *The Frontier in American History*, New York: Holt, Rinehart, Winston, 1962

INDEX

ABOUT THE AUTHOR

Barbara Habenstreit was born and grew up in New York City. She attended the Bronx High School of Science and City College, where she majored in government and put out the student newspaper, *The Campus*. After graduation she worked as a reporter and editor for a weekly newspaper in the city and as a writer for a national trade publication. She received a master's degree in political science and international relations from Long Island University, then taught at the University for a short time before becoming a free lance writer. She is married to Abraham Habenstreit, assistant to the President at Staten Island Community College of the City University. They have a son, David, and a daughter, Shelly, and live in the Fort Green section of Brooklyn.